CONTENTS

CHAPTER 1

Getting There from Here: Leadership and Change

Change is inevitable.
Excerpt from a vending machine.
—bumper sticker wisdom

I had just finished delivering a written report to a congregation that had asked me to work with them because they were experiencing quite a bit of difficulty. I had interviewed most of the active members and had returned to talk with them about what I had learned and to suggest steps they might take to address their problems.

With a clearly pained expression, one woman stated, "What you're saying, Gil, is that we old dogs are going to have to learn new tricks. Is that right?" This was obviously not a comforting idea to her and her husband, who sat next to her. His questions suggested they were not pleased that I had not simply identified who the "guilty" parties were and told them how to return the situation to the way things used to be.

The meeting soon came to an end, and within minutes one of the members of the governing board walked up to me and quietly said, "Thank God, this report might finally get us unstuck and moving on the things we really need to be talking about."

It is not unusual to have these two voices in one congregation (often on one board or committee). They live side by side in our congregations, and leaders are challenged to learn how to listen to both, learn from both, and manage change in a time and culture that demands it, without forcing anyone into win/lose positions.

This is not a book about where your congregation is going. It is a book about how leaders can help your congregation get there.

That is not at all a subtle distinction. Leaders of congregations today need to develop the calmness of spirit and the skills and tools that address the needs of the congregation in the midst of change. Often leaders will not be able to define clearly the end destination of the journey. William Bridges in his recent books *Transitions* and *Managing Transitions* makes the point convincingly that managing change is not just about finding the new spot where you and your congregation are supposed to end up. Rather, it is often more critical to attend to and understand the steps and stages of the transition period that will, in fact, get us to a destination.

It may be neither possible nor sufficient for our congregations today to focus clearly on the goals or destination of our ministry. The environment in which we do ministry is both complex and constantly changing, which does not permit a simple and straightforward movement toward goals. People need help with the change process itself. Although this is not a new idea to leaders who have been working with congregations for the past several years, it certainly is a challenge quite different from those that faced leaders a generation ago.

Yet as far back as 1960 Thomas Merton published a little book called *Bread for the Wilderness*. The title of the book came from the Gospel story in Mark 8 in which Jesus instructed the disciples to feed the great crowd of people who had gathered for three days to listen to him. The disciples asked, "How can one feed these people with bread here in the wilderness?" Merton's response to that question was this book on the Psalms, which he offered as nourishment for the inner life of faith for those who deal with the mix and the mess of the journey. Merton observed that in truly creative times, which prompt new behaviors and new forms of ministry, what we often need from our God, and what our congregations often need from their leaders, is not a quick map to the final destination, the promised land, but "bread for the wilderness"—sustenance and strategies to help us find our ways.

Change

We are in a time of great change. We are facing changes not only in our congregations, but in our families, our work places, our government, our schools—and the list goes on. We are told that this is a time of shifting "paradigms." The dictionary defines paradigm as a pattern, an example, or a model. These paradigms are at the very heart of our understanding of life, and times of great change like we are going through test our very assumptions about life. (My wife, who works in a hospital that is being bought out by a much larger health care conglomerate and whose assumptions about work and career shift and shake as each piece of news comes in, has warned me that if she catches me using the "paradigm" word once again, I'll be eating alone for a week!)

But we are experiencing such large and encompassing "paradigmatic" shifts that the very assumptions on which we base our daily behavior are changing in often confusing ways. Take a quick look at the depth of the change that we are currently living in:

• *The world of sciences*: The very assumption that science would enable us to understand and control the world has been challenged. Fritjof Capra was one of the earlier voices who introduced the learnings of the new sciences, particularly quantum physics, and their new lenses for looking at the world. We used to think of science as mechanical and assumed that if you reduce everything to its component parts, you will be able to understand and "fix" it.[1] Our beliefs about the "mechanical" nature of our universe have been the foundation of our sciences, and Capra is very willing to admit that they have been the basis on which we have sent people to the moon and made discoveries and advances in medicine and a multitude of other areas. To look at the world *only* as a "machine," however, can lead us to false or incomplete conclusions as well. These old assumptions can be very limiting.

• The older mechanical paradigm has implications much closer to home for those of us in congregations. When we use and look at our clergy as "interchangeable parts" in the "machine" of a congregation, we quite often end up changing the clergy but keeping whatever problems we might have. We live with repeat performances of a problem that is much more organic and integral to the very fabric of the congregation and that just gets played out in new versions as we move to the next priest, pastor, or rabbi—the next interchangeable part.

•   *The world of institutions:* The modern American army has been transformed because it has been forced to confront its no-longer work-able assumptions about the possibilities of a "cold war." That reality was changed in November 1989 as the Berlin Wall was torn down by crowds of civilians. Gordon Sullivan, 32nd Chief of Staff of the United States Army, and Michael Harper, director of the CSA Staff Group, describe the shift in paradigm that they faced as they moved from "a bureaucratic industrial society" to an "information society."[2] Because it no longer needs to be staffed and structured to meet the threats of conventional or nuclear war that were possible consequences of the cold war standoff, the army needed to become much smaller and quicker in order to re-spond in an age that moves with the quickness of information technol-ogy.

•   Again, an example of a similar shift closer to home is that congre-gations with problems can no longer look outside themselves to the re-gional, synod, presbytery, or conference office to get a hierarchical, bu-reaucratic "answer" that will fit everyone. Instead, congregations need to learn how to assess their own situation and learn how to experiment in the uniqueness of their own setting. This is quite a significant shift in congregations so used to doing what all other congregations have been doing. How often do you and I still hear leaders (clergy and laity alike) trying to solve a problem in the current moment by starting their sen-tence saying, "Well in my last congregation.…"

It is no wonder that congregations often feel turned upside down as leaders and members search for personal meaning and a way to provide faithful leadership to congregations at a time when our problems are not well understood and the solutions are even more clouded. Loren Mead has pointed out that congregations are living between old and new as-sumptions. A wonderful and remarkable opportunity for congregational leaders is to read and discuss together Mead's argument in *The Once and Future Church: Reinventing the Congregation for a New Mission Frontier.*[3] He sees that congregations are caught between the old as-sumptions of the paradigm of Christendom and the new paradigm of an emerging time.

The Shift from Sameness to Difference

We are in a cultural shift from a time of honoring "sameness" to a time of honoring "difference." Many of us grew up in congregations during a time when we expected our congregation to behave the same way as other congregations of our faith tradition. Much of this expectation was based on our experience of a culture that reinforced sameness. I ask congregational leaders who attend continuing education events I lead how many different types of telephones they could choose from in 1947 if they wanted to get an extra telephone in their house. (Of course, it did not usually occur to people in 1947 that they might need or want more than one phone in a house.) But if you needed a phone, you got a "standard issue" telephone which was black, heavy, with a rotary dial and a wire that attached it to your wall. You got what everybody else got because the assumption was that if you needed a telephone, you needed what everybody else needed. This culture of sameness applied to our homes, our appliances, our social groups, and our congregations. If you were Methodist, you worshipped like all other Methodist churches, using the same liturgy as all other Methodists at 11:00 a.m. on Sunday morning. You had the same administrative groups and meetings on weekday evenings. You had the same Christian education groups, the same Epworth League, the same Women's Society of Christian Service, and you sent your mission dollars to the same denominationally sponsored missionaries. The assumption was that if you were Methodist you did what other Methodists did, and if you were looking for a church, you could (and should) pick from any of the "standard issue" Methodist congregations that were near your home. After all, they were all the same in a one-size-fits-all world.

This uniformity among congregations was the outgrowth of the Christendom paradigm that Mead talked about in the culture of sameness: Congregations were understood to be made up of similar people practicing faith in a similar manner. In fact, he speaks about the purpose of the congregation, in its larger social context, as making good *citizens*. Citizenship itself was supported by the sameness of congregations, which undergirded and underscored the need for people to behave alike. Being a good member of a congregation and being a good citizen or good community participant were understood to be similar, if not identical. The lessons from that time were sufficiently strong that they continue to form many of our current congregational leaders' assumptions. They easily turn to reminiscing about the way things used to be when confronted with a difficult problem today.

We no longer live in a time of sameness, however. We live in a culture that embraces differences. Just as people expect to find telephones in a seemingly unending array of choices, people seeking a shared faith require that congregations offer paths and programs to meet their specific and unique needs and desires. Churches now need to offer worship services specifically designed for the worshippers they hope to attract, short-term task forces that will accommodate the busy lifestyle of members in ways that standing committees cannot, several women's groups that fit the age and interests of their participants, and ways to support mission programs and missionary personnel that have a specific appeal or relationship to this one congregation. We can no longer assume that one United Methodist church will look like or behave like a neighboring United Methodist church. In fact, it is important that each congregation of any faith tradition be able to differentiate itself from other congregations in order to speak to and welcome people who come to the congregation with their individual needs. We no longer believe that one size fits all but that everyone is encouraged to find his or her own size.

The driving assumption about congregations today is that they each have a unique call to ministry, a call very much determined by the congregation's location and ministry with a specific and unique group of individuals, who have specific and unique needs and interests within the greater framework of the faith tradition. Ministry is no longer a matter of doing what we know how to do best. Nor is it adequate for congregations to continue to do what they did last year. The time and the environment continue to change at a pace that requires us constantly to evaluate, to learn anew what our purpose of ministry is, and continually to reinvent the congregation to meet the needs that face us. We need to learn more at every turn before discerning the appropriate next step to take. Can you imagine what this does to planning and budgeting in congregations that are used to just looking at last year and asking, "What next?"

This shift from honoring sameness to honoring difference is a change that is as much cultural as it is congregational. In today's culture, which so consistently honors differences, even buying an appliance is not simple any more. Typically, if you go to a store to buy a refrigerator—and you happen to be in a store that actually still has salespeople—

the salesperson will quite naturally want and need to learn about *you* before beginning the conversation about the kind of refrigerator you want to buy. By learning about you, the salesperson will then be able to educate you about what you need in refrigerators—the amount of storage area; top-and-bottom or side-by-side doors; water, juice, or ice access from the front door panel, and on and on. For those of us who do not always shop where there are salespeople, magazines and publications such as *Consumer Reports* educate us and help us through the complex choices available in our culture of differences.

If it takes such work to buy a refrigerator, which is a fairly basic and standard part of our homes, consider what it takes to understand a congregation and its specific call to ministry. In our time, people wonder about their specific faith and family needs, and they will expect congregations to honor these needs.

Because of the complexity of our lives, congregations will be traveling different directions and will experiment with new and different forms of congregational life and ministry as they seek to share faith with people in this time of changing assumptions and paradigms. Researcher Nancy Ammerman from Hartford Seminary believes there is a good measure of experimentation and adaptation going on already within congregations because of the new realities.[4] She indicates that congregations in which leaders know well the histories, stories, and myths of the congregations will be helped through the time of change by their sensitivity to their uniqueness. Congregations that are comfortable handling conflict (the differences brought to them by their members) will find this skill helps them to manage transition. (She has also found that not all congregations are able to manage transition; some will be caught in unchangeable decline and death.) But her research, along with the research and experience of the Alban Institute and research by a number of major mainline denominations, continues to underscore the reality that there will be lots of different ministry "destinations" for our congregations in the next chapter of our histories.

We can no longer assume that all (or many) congregations are heading in the same direction. And we can no longer hope that denominational or parachurch programs or solutions can be counted on to solve our congregational dilemmas. In fact, the major conclusion of extensive work that was done by three national Lutheran church bodies and Aid Association for Lutherans (the "Church Membership Initiative" project) highlights the uniqueness of each congregation and the need for a unique ministry response from each congregation. In a booklet summarizing the findings of primary research that was conducted over a period of six years, researchers concluded, "Solutions are found within *individual, motivated congregations taken one at a time*" (emphasis added).[5]

So congregational leaders need to accept that, while it may be possible to learn from other congregations and from the programs many congregational workers are developing, the path of ministry is necessarily one in which each congregation and its leaders are going to have to develop their own learnings and make their own decisions in this culture of differences. There are no magic or standard solutions available in this time of change that honors differences. As I often tell congregations I am working with, there is no cookbook to follow, no established rules that will get us there. That is true of any organization, not just congregations. When talking about the redevelopment of the army, Sullivan and Harper said:

> The challenge for the leader is not to get "it" exactly right, because there is not an "it." The challenge is to become "good enough": good enough to seize and exploit developing opportunities, good enough to deploy your forces more rapidly than competitors, good enough to get it "about right" in execution.[6]

Similarly, in an article about the twenty-first-century CEO, one major consulting group is very clear that the attribute that will make the difference in the corporate world is not the ability to come up with "the answer" but the ability to be *organizationally agile* enough to find the right next step. "Passion for the business, alertness to opportunity, focus on speed and responsiveness, willingness to experiment with things as fundamental as distributions channels—these are characteristics of an agile organization."[7]

Of course, congregations are not the army. And congregations are not businesses. Despite the economic realities that must be attended to and the fiduciary responsibility of board members, the purpose of a congregation cannot be compared to the military or management. Nonetheless, the need to find our own path and the fact that we cannot lay claim to "the answer" that fits all congregations is a situation we share with other institutions, corporations, and systems in this time of great change.

What, then, is the role of congregational leaders? It is to be faithful to the journey—to the challenge, the experimentation, the trial and error of ministry in a culture of change. And it is to be responsive. In Matthew 4 we read that Jesus turned to potential followers and simply said, "Follow me, and I will make you fish for people," and the potential disciples "immediately" left their nets and followed him. There were no questions asked and no clear promises given about where the trip would take them.

We do not live in a time of clear answers; we live in a time when leaders will need to use discernment and experimentation to guide their congregations through changes. I am continually helped by one of my favorite definitions of discernment in a faith community: "Discernment can be like driving an automobile at night; the headlights cast only enough light for us to see the next small bit of road immediately in front of us. Ultimately discernment requires our willingness to act in faith on our sense of what God wants us to do."[8]

Two Fears in Congregations

It has long been recognized that fear paralyzes organizations as much as it paralyzes individuals. If leaders of congregations are responsible for motivating and organizing a process of faithful discernment without being able to describe and define the results before the journey begins, the leaders need to understand and to cope with the fear that could paralyze the congregational system.

Two essential fears face our congregations:

• the fear of too much change, and
• the fear of too little change.

Too Much Change

The fear of too much change is the fear of being out of control. As congregations look ahead to a time when they may be worshiping with a different order of worship, a new style of music, or leadership roles that do not follow clear and distinct clergy/laity divisions, the fear is that something important will be lost in the process. "Let's not throw out the baby with the bath water!" is the cry frequently heard from those who fear that change will grow out of hand. Our fears, often shared by leaders and members alike, focus on the possibility that we will lose something important to us or that we will feel uncomfortable.

We should not be particularly surprised by this reaction against change. As we will discuss later, this frequently encountered reaction—efforts to slow down or to stop change—has natural and healthy roots, according to a systems understanding of a congregation. The effort to minimize change, or to keep it from going out of control, is not the product of mean-spirited and uncaring people (although sadly it can be experienced in mean-spirited and uncaring ways.) It is, in fact, often the effort of a congregational or institutional system trying to keep itself in balance.

When leaders are confronted with resistance to the change they are proposing, they often, quite naturally, take the opposition personally. The pastor worries about why some key people in the congregation "don't like me any more." Lay leaders worry that the reaction to their leadership may interrupt relationships they have come to trust and value. As difficult as it is, clergy and lay leaders alike need to separate their personal feelings from the experience of resistance to their efforts, and they need to realize that a natural, expected reaction of any system to the introduction of change or uncertainty is the fear that things will spin out of control and that something valuable will be lost.

It may be helpful for leaders to play a little game that reminds us that resistance is a natural response to change and that we need to work through this response to find the treasures that can await us on the other side. This game is an opportunity to play with an idea for a bit, without having to be overly serious or produce any wisdom. It frees us to look at our immediate situation from a new perspective. Simply invite two or three other leaders in your congregation (perhaps from a planning team or a governing board) to join you in a ten-minute structured conversation like the following:

A Game   –

(ten minutes total)

"It is the nature of people as they grow older to protest against change, particularly change for the better."
—John Steinbeck, author

1. Ask group members to read this quote. Then invite them to think of as many examples as possible of changes for the better in the following arenas that were initially protested by people. *(four minutes)*

- in the workplace
- in the field of entertainment
- in the church

2. With the remaining six minutes, discuss what values and contributions we would have missed if these changes had not been made. *(six minutes)*

Too Little Change

One fear is of too much change, and the matching counter-fear is of not enough change—or the inability to get change started. A consultant colleague of mine uses the wonderful expression, "You can't steer a parked car!" Many leaders in congregations, and a good number of impatient members, are often very concerned that leaders will not be able to bring about change because of the deeply rooted traditions and long-practiced behaviors that guide many of our congregations. The concern is legitimate. Traditions and practiced behavior are strong determinants of resistance to change in any organization.

Again, congregations are not alone in facing seemingly impossible change. At some level, it is simply the way of the world to resist change. Consider this curiosity: The standard U.S. railroad gauge, the distance between rails, is 4 ft. 8.5 in.—an exceedingly odd measurement for standardization. Tracing back, we find the measurement was brought to

12

The Alban Institute

the United States by English expatriates, who built the American railroads the way they were built in England. And tracing that history, we find the same standard was copied by the English railroad people to match the prerailroad tramways. That standard, in turn, conforms to the jigs and tools for building wagons, which used the same wheel spacing. And that spacing conformed to the spacing of old wheel ruts on old long-distance roads, because wheels and axle would be broken if they did not ride smoothly in the well-established ruts. And the ruts were developed through the use of these long-distance roads, constructed by imperial Rome for their legions and war chariots, which were built to standard specifications. The conclusion is that the 1997 U.S. standard railroad gauge of 4 ft. 8.5 in. is based on the original specifications of the imperial Roman army war chariot.[9] Can you imagine trying to change that tradition!

Yet consider the effect in our own faith communities of not trying to change. In a presentation to a small group of clergy, Leonard Sweet, Dean of Drew University Theological School, talked about his young son, who would come home from school with a friend, turn on the TV in one room, turn music on in another room, flop down with his friend in front of the computer and, using their computer's joy sticks, in minutes become deeply involved in a CD-ROM game that explored the human body in great detail. Sweet paused to reflect that his son was living in a stimulus-rich world. The youngster was not bothered or confused by music and TV programming overlapping while he and his friend were engaged in a third activity. In fact, if the telephone rang, the two young people would simply add the phone to the rest of the stimulation with which they were surrounded; they would not even think about turning anything off in order to have the conversation. Beyond that, Sweet noted, his son and his friend were engaged in a computer *game* that was as inviting as it was educational, and that learning was being done on a collaborative basis as the two friends worked together to find their way through the graphics and the detailed information about the body.

And then, noted Sweet, following congregational tradition, his son goes to Sunday school, where he is presented with a one-dimensional flannelgraph board and students are told to sit quietly in rows and not interact with one another or the teacher. A noninteractive Bible story is told, and he is supposed to simply remember the story and do little else with it. If some of the members of a congregation fear that change will happen too quickly, others fear that it is not happening fast enough to allow the faith to speak to people living in a culture that has rushed past the way many of our congregations share and practice their faith.

This counterpoint of change and nonchange in many of our congregations presents competing challenges, like the ancient Scylla and Charybdis of classical mythology—the rock and the whirlpool between which leaders certainly think they are going to lose their ship.

What's a Leader to Do?

The first thing leaders can do is to relieve themselves of the pressure to come up with the perfect "answer" to an uncertain future that will keep all parties in the congregation "happy." I cannot stress this point too strongly.

Many congregational leaders will be surprised to hear that their task is not to focus on the "happiness" (satisfaction) of the members. They are aware that because congregations are volunteer organizations, members can either quietly slip away or leave under loud protest if their needs and interests are not satisfied by what they find there. Clergy who are financially and relationally dependent upon their congregation are naturally very sensitive to any voices of unhappiness that might threaten their security. Lay leaders, though feeling dependent in different ways from clergy, are also sensitive to unhappiness or dissatisfaction in the congregation that might disrupt their relationships, severely complicate the responsibilities they have assumed in their congregation, or interfere with their own spiritual needs, which brought them to the congregation in the first place. So it is not unnatural for leaders to be highly sensitive to happiness or satisfaction in the congregation and themselves to resist or avoid steps that might disrupt the happiness.

But in a time when the environment is changing rapidly both inside and outside the congregation—when the very makeup of the congregation as well as the surrounding community and culture are changing—the focus on happiness and satisfaction is insufficient and, in the end, damaging. Happiness and satisfaction are very often measures of the status quo. If we say change is the thing that makes the most people the most uncomfortable most of the time, then nonchange is the thing that would make most of the people most comfortable most of the time. Yet a posture of nonchange in an environment of great change is not a position of faithful leadership. It is a formula for disconnecting the congregation from the very culture or community it has been called to address—a formula for decline and eventual death. Leaders must learn new ways to understand their congregations. They must learn to lead change without subjecting every decision and action to the evaluation based on whether people are pleased or happy with the results.

Leadership and Management

One of the helpful distinctions that seems new to many of the participants in continuing education events I lead is between "leadership" and "management." Although both these functions are needed by the congregation, they are not the same and they are not needed in equal measure at all times and circumstances. It is helpful and healthy for clergy and laity who have accepted responsibility in congregations to be clear about when they need to *lead* and when they need to *manage*.

"Managers do things right. Leaders do the right things."[10] This distinction by Warren Bennis and Burt Nanus, well-known consultants and leaders in organizations, expresses well the difference between the two functions of management and leadership. Managers are largely responsible for the stability and the efficient and smooth working of an organization. In congregations, managers are responsible for setting the budget, maintaining and repairing the facilities, making sure volunteers are elected and prepared to fulfill their appointed tasks or roles, providing the necessary resources, and making sure events are scheduled so that committees and groups are not in conflict over space or time.

Leaders are quite different. They do not ask the management question, are we doing things right? They ask the more difficult question, are we doing the right things? Leaders step out into the future to discern what God is calling the congregation to do in the next chapter of its life. Managers are the voice of stability in the congregation (and therefore sensitive to measures of happiness or satisfaction); leaders are the voice of change in the congregation (and more sensitive to measures of purpose and faithfulness).

Make no mistake. Congregations need and depend upon *both* good managers and good leaders. A congregation that overemphasizes management will be stuck in a status quo that will eventually strangle growth and development in a changing environment. A congregation that over-emphasizes leadership will alienate members, by damaging or even removing the trusted behaviors and principles that provide a stable base from which members might take new steps toward change. In large, multi-level, hierarchical organizations, it is very clear who has leadership responsibilities (upper management and CEOs) and who has management responsibilities (middle management and project managers). But in very complex but hierarchically flat organizations like congregations, which have significantly fewer levels of organizational structure, the responsibilities are not as clearly divided. Clergy are often seen as simultaneously responsible for vision (the leadership question: Where are we called to go?) and daily operation (the management question: How do we keep everything operating smoothly?). Governing boards in congregations and key lay leaders, who are looked to as the primary voices of the congregation, are also expected to play both roles.

The dilemma is that the voices of management and the voices of leadership in organizations do not always get along well, because they have different functions or purposes. Consider the vignette Stephen Covey tells about producers, managers, and leaders.

> You can quickly grasp the difference between the two if you envision a group of producers cutting their way through the jungle with machetes. They're the producers, the problem solvers. They're cutting through the undergrowth, clearing it out.
>
> The managers are behind them, sharpening their machetes, writing policy and procedure manuals, holding muscle development programs, bringing in improved technologies and setting up working schedules and compensation programs for machete wielders.
>
> The leader is the one who climbs the tallest tree, surveys the entire situation, and yells, "Wrong jungle!"
>
> But how do the busy, efficient producers and managers often respond? "Shut up! We're making progress."[11]

Can you see that in an era of "sameness" (when it could reasonably be assumed that all congregations of any given faith tradition would be relatively similar, if not resolutely the same, in worship, programs, and organization) people would largely depend upon the practice of management? Our congregational leaders over the past generations were asked

to provide effective management. They asked, appropriately: Are we
being effective stewards of our resources? Are we satisfying the basic
needs of people who come to one of our churches? Are things going
smoothly? In an era of "difference," however, the greater need is for
leadership. All congregations need a healthy and appropriate balance
between management and leadership, but when congregations need to
learn new things and confront new realities, they need a greater measure
of leadership. Visioning questions need to be addressed: Who are we?
What ministry are we called to give? These two questions are the congregational equivalents of the corporate questions: What business are we
in? What do we need to learn in order to prepare ourselves for what we
are called to do?

The criteria by which we measure management are satisfaction and
happiness (Are things going smoothly? Are we covering the bases?). The
criteria by which we measure leadership must be quite different. We
need to ask different questions about our ministry, such as: Is it faithful
to our understanding of our purpose? Is it responsive to a viable future?
Is it open to people who are not yet here and not yet part of our congregation? Is it consistent with our core values? Does the change we are
considering help us to respond to the previous questions? Will change
help us to overcome the barriers to a viable future that we have been
seeking?

The fact that effective leadership is not measured by satisfaction
and happiness is difficult for congregational leaders, who often want to
deal with members' problems and make things go smoothly. That is why
often the first step to leading change in the congregation is for the leaders themselves to understand this essential difference between management and leadership and to prepare themselves for the quite different
and less immediately satisfying role of leader.

A Word about Leadership

In a time of great change, leaders' responsibilities and roles are not
about providing the answers or solutions their organizations are seeking.
Leadership does not mean a wise or powerful individual imposes on others a vision or an "answer." Our American cultural mythology is full of
stories about strong and wise individuals who ride in to rescue the day in

the style of John Wayne, the Lone Ranger, Lee Iacocca, or Jack Welsh. Our love affair with American individualism supports our telling stories about lone rescuers, and we sometimes believe that is what true leaders do—despite the evidence. This myth makes leading even more difficult for congregational leaders, who often do not see themselves or their personalities in such a mold and who know that they do not have the magic answer in their back pocket.

In fact, leaders are not the ones with irrefutable answers but the ones who can support others and help them ask the right questions. Leaders do as much listening as they do talking. As visions are sought, leaders are the ones who keep the conversation alive and active in the congregation, allowing the vision to be shaped by past history, current practice, and future opportunities and call. They do not announce the conclusions about the future that they have independently reached as much as they enable a responsible discernment of the future by the group.

Leadership is a hot topic today because people in corporations, institutions, and congregations are trying to figure out what their organizations need from them. And the research and anecdotes are getting more instructive all the time. Go browse the business section of your local neighborhood bookstore and you will discover that it is hard not to be rewarded with a good find.

One helpful insight comes from Craig Dykstra, Vice President for Religion with Lilly Endowment Inc., who points out that there are several meanings to the word *vision*.[12] The one we are most familiar with and the one we tend to think of first is "foresight"—the future-oriented capacity to perceive what is not. This is an essential ingredient for moving the congregation toward something to which God calls it. Foresight means being able to look responsibly into the future and to describe changes that would be faithful to the purpose and the call of a congregation.

Too often, however, we short-circuit our full understanding of vision by thinking of it *only* as forecasting. The other meaning Dykstra points to is vision as "perception"—the capacity to perceive realistically what is present. Vision is also the ability to see, and help others to see, the way things actually are. Referring to the writings of English moral philosopher and novelist Iris Murdock, Dykstra points out that perceiving things clearly is not at all a simple or common task and writes: "We do not see very well ... because deep (but usually unnamed) fears distort our perception. Ordinary perception is filtered though anxiety-ridden imaginations, filled with caricatures, bias, conventionality, and wishful thinking. We see mostly what we want to see and are blind to what we are unable or unwilling to let affect us."[13]

Often a cynical or questioning public was frustrated with former President George Bush when he talked about "the vision thing," because what they heard seemed more focused on foresight, which sounded more like fantasy than vision. Leadership requires both senses of vision, both *foresight* and an accurate and a caring *perception* of the current reality. And the essential task of leaders in a time of change is to keep the conversation going between the voices of perception and the voices of foresight in the congregation.

Not long ago I was teaching a continuing education workshop in Wisconsin and experienced a marvelous serendipity that offered a deeper insight into this. I was teaching a course on the leadership and management of congregational revitalization, and in the same conference center another consultant was working on leadership issues with a group of superintendents and principals of public schools. Both groups had opportunity to wander around during breaks and free time. On the second day members of the group I was leading began to come back from visits with members of the other group carrying "purloined" handouts. Members of our group were fascinated that the superintendents and principals were wrestling with exactly the same issues we were working with as clergy and lay leaders of congregations. By the third day I had bumped into participants from the other group and kidded them that members of my group were scouting them out. "Don't worry," they laughed. "During our breaks some of us come and stand outside your door to listen to what your group is talking about, and at night we come in to copy from your newsprint."

Apart from the fascination that what we are wrestling with as congregational leaders is both interdisciplinary and fundamental to all organizations, one of the gifts of that encounter was the definition of vision that the public school leaders were using. It began, "Vision is a continuous conversation to define clearly the results a group of people want to create."[14] The vision in congregations needs to be about more than the results a group of people want to create. It also has to reflect our discernment of the will of God for our future. But it must grow out of "a continuous conversation." Leadership in our congregations today requires that clergy and lay leaders manage a continuous and healthy conversation between the reality of perception and the possibility of foresight—that they keep the vision alive. Leadership is not about being able to announce the conclusions of the conversation to the congregation in ways that will convince and satisfy everyone. It is about "reading" the congregation and gaining some intuitive or reasoned understanding of how to continue the conversation.

At the heart of this book are tools—ideas, models, lenses to look through—you can use to understand how your congregation is responding or reacting to changes that face them. Based on your understanding of the congregation, you can then make decisions about the most helpful way to continue the conversation of faithful visioning of a yet unclear future. This book incorporates some of the tools I have used in my work with congregations.

A Few Assumptions

Before we look at the tools, however, I want to identify several assumptions or guidelines that need to be honored as we work with congregations facing change. I invite you to consider these assumptions and to explore your reaction to them as a leader who will undoubtedly face the ongoing task of helping to negotiate changes facing your congregation in this time of wonderful opportunities.

1. We are seeking new learnings, not following old rules.

This assumption was explored a bit above, but it is worth repeating here because we need to pay as much, or more, attention to how we help our congregations negotiate the changes that face them than to our ability to "deliver them safely on the other side." This is a time for you as a leader to support adult learning in the search for new ways.

The four components of the adult learning cycle are as follows:

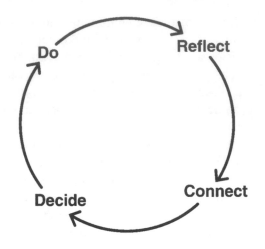

Adults learn best when they pause after *doing* something to *reflect* on what they just did and what they learned from it. This new learning is enriched when they then *connect* their new learnings with previous experiences and insights that can help to inform their reflection on what they just did. Then with this new learning in place they make a *decision* about next steps and then implement *(do)* those steps.

The dilemma many of our congregations face is that we have been practicing management and seeking stability for so long that we spend almost all of our time on the left half of the cycle, simply asking our leaders to do and decide over and over again without finding time and opportunity to reflect and connect. Board members often are asked to pack six or more decisions into one night and then to struggle to identify the person who will be the "doer" and make it happen before the next board meeting.

In a time of sameness, such strategies tend to work because the basic issue managers are trying to work with is how to make things go smoothly. And in stable periods, much of management centers on doing again what has been done in the past. Management requires little reflection or connecting in search of new learnings. But in times of great change, when leadership is needed and there are no ground rules about next steps, the left-hand side of the cycle must be informed by the right-hand half of reflecting and connecting. In fact, many congregations are experiencing so much change that their governing boards and leaders need to spend more of their time and energy on the right side of the cycle than on the left.

Because there is no recipe to get us through change, and our future faithfulness depends on new learnings, congregational leaders need to spend time "learning" about their perception and foresight without feeling disappointed if the meeting does not include decisions. Meeting in some space other than the board room to talk, study, and pray about the congregation and its future—without the visible reminders of the board room to make them feel guilty about not making decisions—can bear much fruit.

2. Change will produce conflict, which is good and not to be avoided.

Conflict is "two or more ideas in the same place at the same time." Conflict is not necessarily a "fight." But it is the engagement and working out of differences. Working with the different ideas that produce conflict is good in a time of change. If your congregation and the leaders of your congregation have only *one* idea, you are probably in trouble if you are facing a time that requires adaptability and experimentation. An old truism says, "When we don't know what else to do, we do what we know." Too often "what we know" is the only idea a congregation has about its present and its future. But in a time of change, more than one idea is good. Out of the "conflict" of more than one idea comes energy, motivation, clarity, and direction. Without such conflict, which is the engagement of differences, it is very hard to responsibly meet a changing future.

Now this assumption suggests that our congregational leaders and members need to be better prepared to respond to more than one idea. All too often people have a very limited repertoire for dealing with differences. They center their efforts on persuasion and winning. In the final chapter of this book, I will offer some ideas about responsible behavior in congregations as communities of faith during times of change. Along with learning about conflict management, clergy and lay leaders need to be aware of their own comfort and personal preferences when dealing with two or more ideas in the congregation. This is a part of the larger need for congregational leaders to be informed about and trained in managing conflict.

3. We need to appreciate experimentation and failure.

Our congregational culture, learned in a time of stability and sameness, has trained us to assume that everything we try in our congregations must not "fail." Far too often we evaluate efforts by counting the number of people involved or the dollars raised or spent. Far too often we fail to evaluate efforts by asking, What have we learned?

Learning requires the hard work of analysis, discussion, and discernment. This learning, often referred to as the "up-front" work, can lead to effective action later. The willingness to experiment with new programs or approaches will provide new information, which will in turn support the learning necessary in a time of change. Using resources to experiment and to gather information is not wasted, it is not a failure, if the information is used for learning in order to further discern the future. Congregations need to be able to follow the lead of other organizations and institutions in valuing, and celebrating, experiments and failures in their ministry. In a time when the people and dollar resources available to congregations are increasingly shrinking, we need to help people understand that experimentation is not a waste of time and dollars. Responsible experiments and valuable failures are those that lead to further insights about what God is asking of us.

4. Leadership is essentially a spiritual issue.

Congregations are faith communities. Their ongoing purpose is to introduce people to a relationship with God through the disciplines of their faith tradition, which can be life changing. Their corporate purpose is ultimately to be faithful to the call of God within the understanding of their faith tradition.

This book will try to blend the understandings of our faith traditions with the learnings of the human social sciences and the experience of leaders in corporations and institutional settings such as government, hospitals, and universities, as well as in congregations. Ours is a time in which people are seeking and learning across many of the fences and the barriers, such as the self-contained disciplines of the university or the divisions between the sacred and the secular, that we used to so willingly honor. This interdisciplinary effort is one of the richest gifts and opportunities of our age.

Nonetheless, the congregation is a *faith* community and will ultimately find its place by clearly shaping its spirit, not its structure or its
programs. Leaders in congregations need to remember that some of their
most essential learnings will come from their Bible study and not from
their budget reports. Leaders in congregations need to understand that
the freedom they seek in order to move with confidence into the future
will come from the strength of their spirit and not from their track record
with attendance or financial giving.

In fact, while listed as the last of the assumptions to be honored by
leaders in congregations, this assumption about the spiritual nature of
the work of leaders is perhaps the most critical. In the next chapter we
will explore this spiritual nature of leadership.

Exercises for Leaders

The following exercises can certainly be done by the reader alone. You will probably learn more, however, if you do the exercises with several other leaders and use your responses as a basis for further conversation about leadership in a time of change. Similar exercises are provided at the end of each chapter.

1. Discuss the following questions:

• What excites you about being called to be a leader of your congregation in this time of change?
• What frightens or concerns you about being called to be a leader of your congregation in this time of change?
• What new behaviors or practices of leadership might you need to consider, and what old practices or behaviors might you need to reconsider so you can effectively lead your congregation into the future?
• What might you have to learn in order to be a faithful leader of your congregation?

2.
A. Based on the four guiding assumptions at the end of this chapter, assess yourself on the following scales.

X   Place an *X* on the scale to indicate how strongly you agree or disagree with the assumption.
L   Place an *L* on the scale to indicate how strongly you think the *core leaders* of your congregation agree or disagree with the assumption.
C   Place a *C* on the scale to indicate how strongly you think the *members of your congregation* agree or disagree with the assumption.

1. We will need to commit time and energy to reflecting on and connecting with our experiences as a congregation as well as to deciding and doing.

1	2	3	4	5
Agree				Disagree

2. Conflict (the presence of two or more ideas) is essential to our future.

1	2	3	4	5
Agree				Disagree

3. We need to appreciate experimentation and failure as ways to learn more about our ministry.

1	2	3	4	5
Agree				Disagree

4. We need to pay attention to and learn more about our spiritual lives if we are to provide leadership for our congregation.

1	2	3	4	5
Agree				Disagree

B. Draw the above four scales on a piece of newsprint and invite all participants to place their *X's*, *L's*, and *C's* on the appropriate scales. As a group, identify and discuss the patterns in your responses. What views do you share? Where do you differ?

CHAPTER 2

A Place in the Story: The Spiritual Assumptions of Leaders

O God, whose mercy is ever faithful and ever sure,
who art our refuge and our strength in time of trouble,
visit us, we beseech thee—for we are a people in trouble.
We need a hope that is made wise by experience
and is undaunted by disappointment.
We need an anxiety about the future
that shows us new ways to look at new things
but does not unnerve us.
—from a prayer by William Sloane Coffin Jr.

The governing board asked me to work with them for a day because they discovered they found it hard to work with each other every year from October to January—budget time. They were puzzled about what was going on, because the rest of the year went smoothly and they were enthusiastic about their church and one another. But every budget season, the tension mounted. They were even beginning to question quietly the leadership of the senior clergy, who did not seem quite able to get them through these rough spots.

I was as puzzled as they were. We looked at changes they faced, and we shared differences. The information they shared all seemed helpful and informative—but not to the point.

Then in the afternoon I asked them to break into three small groups, each with a separate task. One group was asked to identify the biblical story they thought their board or their congregation was living out at that time. In other words, if they were to place themselves in the larger biblical story, where would they find themselves? What part of the biblical record belonged to them?

*The tasks took about an hour and a half. There was lots of kid-
ding in the Bible story group—that there were not enough Bibles to go
around and that I had not given them enough time to read through the
whole Bible to figure out which story was theirs. Of the three groups,
however, this was the one that clearly had most of the energy. They
were challenged by the task and worked hard at it.*

*When the full group gathered, the Bible story subgroup an-
nounced confidently that they had found themselves. "We are the story
of Mary and Martha," they explained. (See Luke 10:38-42). "When
Jesus visited Mary and Martha, Martha complained that Mary just sat
and listened to him talking about faith while she was busy with the
tasks of caring for him as a guest. That's just like us," they said. "Some
of us are concerned about the tasks of raising money and fixing the
building and want to talk about repair projects and monthly finance
statements. But others of us are concerned about what we are doing
about members' faith and want to talk about programs and mission
trips. Each of us is afraid the other side is going to use up all the time
and money. No wonder we have trouble at budget time.We are Mary
and Martha. Some of us are worried about doing the dishes, and others just want to go and talk with Jesus."*

*The change in the group was subtle, but it was obvious bells were
ringing, lights were going on, and people were having an "aha" experience. The rest of the afternoon was spent exploring the board's
Mary-and-Martha polarity, and the need for both Mary and Martha to
feel honored and cared for, without pitting Mary and Martha against
each other. By the end of the day they had agreed they would build
their agenda to honor each side of the board. They would structure
each meeting to include time for a "Mary conversation" and separate
time for a "Martha conversation." They found their place in the story,
and they wanted to live it.*

The Burden of Leadership

To be a leader in a congregation in a time of change requires a willingness to confront spiritual questions. The tasks of leading are increasingly
difficult, because old solutions more frequently seem not to fit new situations. The purpose and meaning of leading in congregations has become

increasingly problematic as well. Are leaders called to lead congregations out of problems and back to strength? Or is the present state of a congregation not a problem but a step toward an open future, the new thing God is doing? Deciding which attitude to adopt is an act of faith. Choosing which assumption to live by may be the most important act of leadership that will shape our congregations for the future.

To a large extent our leaders are tired of continuously solving problems and frustrated that they are held responsible for things beyond their control. In his work with governing boards, Chuck Olsen helps leaders transform themselves from decision-making managers into spiritual leaders. Olsen talks about the frustration that he continually hears lay leaders register.[1] Part of his dismay is that it is not uncommon for congregational leaders to become *less active* rather than more active in their congregations when their term of office is completed and they move off of a board or committee. The haunting question that ought not be passed by too quickly is, What does the exercise of leadership do to the spiritual life of our people if it distances them from the congregation rather than drawing them into the community?

Clearly leadership is a burden for our laity, but it also tends to weigh down clergy at all levels. Where once the office of bishop was cherished, it now seems to be draining. In the past eighteen months I have had multiple conversations with active bishops who confide that they are anxiously waiting for retirement to arrive so they can step out of a position they value highly but in which they feel beleaguered.

A moment in which this pain struck me personally was when I was with a colleague and friend who for many years had served as a model of ministry for me. I truly respect him and the decisions and choices he has made in his ministry over the years. I was asked to be the master of ceremonies for the denominational retirement banquet in the conference where he served churches. So I telephoned each of the dozen retirees who would be honored and a number of their friends and family to prepare myself with the jokes and the stories I would need to introduce these people in fun ways that would still honor them. We had a lot of good laughs at the retirement dinner. But in my telephone conversation with my friend, who was also retiring, we reminisced about his years as a clergyperson. With pain that I still feel, he ended with a regret: that the church had grown weaker and had diminished "on his watch." He was referring to the denominational decline that had been going on for over thirty years and that had been reflected in most of the congregations in his judicatory. He was personalizing a common experience and wondering aloud about his faithfulness, which he measured only by the number of people who came to his churches at the end of his ministry compared to the number who came when he was first starting. There was little I could say to reassure him.

What are our assumptions about what is happening to our congregations in this time of change? What are our assumptions about what God is doing in this confusing time facing so many of our congregations? Have we been living through a time of great problems or new opportunities? Is the glass half empty at this point, or half full? Are we optimist or pessimist—remnant or profligate? Most of us find that we have to decide which attitude to adopt and what assumptions to make because there is too much evidence of difficulties, diminished strength, and forced change facing our congregations. And it has been easy for many to interpret the evidence as bad news. For example:

Declining Membership

Mainline denominations have consistently been reporting a decline in membership and attendance at worship over the past twenty to thirty years and have been reporting a decline in their membership as a percentage of the American population over the past thirty to forty years. The trends have been substantial and very difficult to reverse. Denominational trends are mirrored in the long-term decline of many local congregations. The average age of members of many congregations is getting older, and congregational members tend to be older than most of the communities that surround their congregations. Though members continue to financially support the congregation, adequate financial resources are less available to a good percentage of congregations that now have fewer people to share the financial responsibilities. In addition, the dollar has less buying power and members have more claims on their available resources.

For example, although not at all in a desperate situation, one small Episcopal congregation I recently worked with was faced with a difficult decision when their rector, who had been with them for a substantial period of time, was leaving. They are in a historic east coast town that has had very little growth. But through intentional efforts over the years, they have held their own and perhaps even grown a little. Their resources are growing thin, however, and they are wondering what to do about calling their next rector. Do they call a part-time clergyperson, which they could easily afford, and preserve the endowment fund they depend upon to maintain their historic building? If they do, they are sure they will not attract new and younger members, because they have learned that growth is slow and deliberate and takes more energy than the laity can manage by themselves. Or do they use income from their endowment investments to call and support a full-time rector to help maintain the strength they have worked diligently to gain—and if so, what does that suggest about future care and development of their facilities? It is a simple story repeated countless times in countless congregations.

A Missing Generation

Many congregations today are missing a generation. When looking at the tenure of members—the length of time that people have been a member of a particular congregation—more and more congregations have a fairly large cluster of people who have been members for a relatively long period of time, such as twenty or more years. And increasingly congregations have a fairly large cluster of people who are short-termed members of ten years or less. But often these congregations have a dearth of people in the ten- to twenty-year category, which has made it difficult over the years to pass on leadership simply by handing on the responsibility to the people next in line. In many congregations the missing generation has interrupted the smooth flow.

The result is that in an increasing number of congregations, long-tenured members are trying to pass on the customs and responsibilities to short-tenured members but are not comfortable doing so. Congregations discover that the two groups of members share neither interest in nor understanding of some of the long-held practices of the congregation, nor do they have the same needs or expectations of membership in the congregation. The desire to be part of a community of faith is the same in both groups of members, but the way in which they hope to practice their faith is quite different. They argue and feel uncomfortable with one another. But they feel bad about themselves when they do that, because these old and new members in many ways seem so much alike, and their differences are very subtle and often hidden from each other.

For example, it is not unusual to see discomfort growing in worship in such settings. One Baptist congregation in a metropolitan area was very pleased to have younger families joining the church. But some of the long-tenured members were upset when others in the congregation applauded the children after they sang an anthem in the children's choir. "What do I do?" asked one member, who felt caught in the middle. "I really feel like clapping, and I think the children need the encouragement. But I also know I'm breaking my father's heart. He is standing right next to me and hates to hear clapping in church." Family against family, tenured members feel uncomfortable with recent arrivals, and vice versa.

Old Traditions, New Members

Some might think growing congregations in growing communities are beyond these dilemmas. But it is not uncommon for congregations to want *growth* but not to want *change* (not realizing that the two are inseparable) and to have to wrestle with their calling and self-understanding when growth happens.

For example, the elders of a relatively large Mennonite congregation were in a dilemma, having heard a considerable number of complaints from members about the new people who had been joining the congregation. It seemed that the new members attended worship regularly, were supportive with both their money and their volunteer time, and actively participated in the programs of the church. In fact, it seemed that the new members liked and were involved in everything about their new church. Everything, that is, except the traditional Mennonite lifestyle. The result seemed to be that the new members were changing the traditions of the congregation by not adopting a number of the practices of the plain lifestyle, more than the traditions of the faith were changing the new members.

What were the elders to do? Was this congregation called to evangelize and welcome new people to the faith? Or was it called to maintain and pass on a historic faith tradition, which included certain clear and uniform lifestyle expectations as part of the faith practice? Clearly what the elders had been learning up to that point was that you cannot have it both ways.

There are a host of other dividing issues and experiences being encountered in congregations today and countless other congregational stories could be offered as examples. Responding to situations like these will require acts of faith to test the assumptions and attitudes leaders hold. Is it good or bad news that an Episcopal vestry in a small town is feeling cornered into making a choice between their facility and a full-time rector? Does the tension between father and son over applause in worship have purpose, or will it only divide them? Is it good news or bad news that the elders of a congregation are placed in a situation where they have to choose between the voice of tradition and the opportunity of evangelism in calling more people from the community to membership in their congregation? In fact, the key questions facing leaders today may not center so much on what they *do* in situations like these. Rather, the decisive questions may more appropriately be about what the leaders *believe* or *assume* about the situations facing them.

The Assumption That We Have Problems

If we believe the tensions and dilemmas that I have been pointing to are *problems*, then we will treat them as problems and we will search for solutions. We are linear thinkers and we have been well taught that if we have a problem, we should solve it; if something is wrong, we should make it right ; if something is broken, we should fix it. We work with a mental model that has been taught in our culture for hundreds of years:

PROBLEM ⇨ SOLUTION ⇨ IMPLEMENTATION

For us, problems need solutions. And our congregational leaders work very hard at coming up with solutions to the problems they face and the complaints they receive. The problem-solving methodology has limited effectiveness, however, when we face issues over which we have limited or no control. It has been estimated by those who research and work with congregations that 50 to 60 percent of the variables affecting congregations are outside the control of congregational leaders.² Imagine, then, the frustration leaders feel when they assume they are responsible for finding solutions and bringing all problems to resolution when so little is under their control.

Psychologist Murray Bowen has described the environment we live in as filled with free-floating anxiety. What he means is that the world we experience is not always comfortable for us and offers continual challenges and disappointments. There are times, however, when the free-floating anxiety begins to build and pressure increases. When problems are identified and there is no path to resolution, the anxiety builds until it finds focus, and then the anxiety tends to strike like lightning to discharge itself. This is an apt description of the increasing anxiety and the ineffective results of many problem-solving attempts in many of our congregations. Leaders increasingly use their problem-solving skills to solve problems that do not have solutions.

The increase in anxiety prompts people in our congregations to search for *what* is wrong. When they do not find clear and agreeable answers, they quickly try to determine *who* is wrong. In difficult times the search for someone to blame is swift. One of the basic principles of conflict management is to separate the people from the issues and to teach folks how to talk about and address change focused on the issues, not on the people.³ This is hard and often feels like unnatural work, because we want to know what is wrong and who is responsible. Not always equipped to make the distinction between people and issues, members of congregations commonly blame leaders for not solving problems that actually have no clear and direct solution. But the assumption that we face "problems" brings with it the assumption that leaders have "solutions," and if we have not found the solutions and implemented them, then the assumption is that someone must be to blame.

People naturally need to find a solution and blame someone. They also seem to have a natural impulse simply to *do* something about an uncomfortable situation, whether the "doing" is helpful or not. This impulse reminds me of the caricature of people in the midst of a crisis who run around yelling "Do something ! Anything!!" When we assume that we have identified a problem, we want someone to do something about it and we move quickly to action—to fixing it.

Three Quick Fixes

In fact, it is often healthier and more responsible for leaders *not* to try to "fix" their congregation.[4] By seeking quick but inappropriate solutions, leaders tend to add to the discomfort and disequilibrium of their situation and actually subvert the opportunity to address deeper issues they face. Often quick fixes are collusive exercises that are intuitively designed not to bring any real change to the congregation but offer the feeling that something has been done. When congregations get involved in the quick-fix mode of restructuring, they tend to make changes in the "three *Ps*"—people, program, and policy. Let's look at three examples.

People

The most popular people for congregations to change are the clergy. One congregation called a new pastor because they wanted a leader who would reconnect them to the neighborhood in which they lived. They were very clear with their new pastor about their goals. But within the first three months of their new pastor's tenure, there were fourteen incidents in which leaders graciously (and sometimes not so graciously) invited the pastor aside to helpfully explain to her that "this is how we do it here." In other words, they changed the person of their pastor and set new goals that would require a change in congregational behavior but collusively enforced old rules that made it impossible for the new pastor to address the stated goals with any real change.

Program

I once sat with a governing board of thirty people in a congregation that was concerned its rate of growth was not keeping up with the rate of growth in the surrounding community. Ten minutes into the discussion one board member said that he had recently been reading the denominational newsletter and remembered a series of articles about doing ministry with single adults (people never married, or separated). The congregations highlighted in the articles had grown significantly. "I move," he said, ending his speech, "that we begin a ministry to singles as a way of

increasing our growth in membership." There was already a second offered to his motion before I had time to speak. But when I questioned
the group, we discovered that none of the thirty people present was
single. We further discovered that none of the thirty people knew anyone else in the congregation who was single. In fact, only two people
knew anyone in the community around the congregation who was single.

The problem was that this congregation was located in a rather con-
servative rural setting in which single people did not feel comfortable
and therefore did not settle. Married people in the community who became single tended to move away. It was not that others in the community were unkind to them. It was that the orientation of the community
(and of this congregation) was so family centered that people did not
know how to talk with those who did not live in a traditional family setting. Yet this congregation was poised and ready to "do something"
about their situation that would involve time, money, and people with
no possibility of addressing the real issues that made it hard for them to
receive new members. And, undoubtedly, when their effort to minister
to singles failed, the natural tendency would have been for them to want
to know what and who went wrong—and why.

Policy

A small congregation in a major metropolitan area was very concerned
about the number of inactive members on its roles. At a board meeting
in which inactives were discussed, one board member came up with a
policy solution. "At the upcoming election of new leaders, I move we
nominate at least two inactive members to each of our committees. That
way," he said, "they will come out to the meetings and see what is going
on and get reinterested in our congregation and start coming back to
worship." He was well meaning, to be sure. But a committee meeting is
perhaps the very last place a person who has made a decision not to be
active in a congregation will—or should—show up. Yet the rush to "do"
stimulates activity that even quick reflection will show us is not helpful.

Lost Motivation

The rush to do something, to come up with a solution, subverts a solution to the deeper issue at the heart of the congregation. It also *reduces motivation* for members or leaders to stay on the issue and push for substantive change. The fact is that the very act of doing something is satisfying in the problem ➪ solution ➪ implementation model that we are so used to. It initially does not matter that what we are doing is not effective or even directed at the appropriate issue. There is a satisfying feeling of relief that we are finally doing "something." Subsequently the necessary motivation to hang in there and identify the real issue dissipates.

Consider, as an example, the fact that congregations that have active evangelism or membership growth committees tend to grow and include new members at a slower rate and with more difficulty than congregations that do not have such committees. Much of this at first seemingly illogical situation is due to the fact that once a congregation has formed a committee (once they have "done something about our membership problem"), the motivation of the rest of the congregation is dissipated. The feeling is that the issue is addressed and "we" do not have to do any more about it. The responsibility, then, for inviting new people to the congregation, greeting strangers who come to worship, helping people find their spot in the congregation, or integrating new people into the small groups and activities is "left to the committee." Others not on the committee go back to talking only with the people they already know in the congregation.

Our cultural inclination to frame everything as a problem and then to seek a solution has been very effective for much of our history. As noted above, however, seeing everything as a problem may not always be appropriate. If we use only problem-solving skills and assumptions when something else is called for, we may, in fact, end up blaming, scapegoating, and adopting quick fixes—all of which leave people with a false sense of satisfaction and little motivation for change. Yet we so strongly believe leadership is about "problem solving" and "fixing what's broken" that we do not always see that other options are available. It is an old expression: "If all you have is a hammer, everything you see will look like a nail." If your only mode of leadership is to find problems and solve them, then every situation that you face will look like a problem. Perhaps we need other ways to look at what is in front of us.

If Not a Problem, What?

A Game

(five minutes)

Suppose you are the marketing manager for a manufacturing company. You get a call from the president and learn that somehow the corporate inventory system has fouled up, and the company now has $1,000,000 worth of ball bearings it does not need. Furthermore, you cannot return them to the vendor. Your task is to think of things to do with the ball bearings, using them either one at a time or in combination. What are your ideas? In five minutes, list twenty ways to use the surplus ball bearings.
Hints:

- Sell them as level testers.
- Make furniture out of them—like bean bag chairs—to be used in public places. Because they would be heavy, they would not be stolen.
- Serve them as "robot caviar" (when your "home robot" is having friends over).

Like the game in the first chapter, this little game[5] is an opportunity to play with an idea for a bit without having to be overly serious and productive. It frees us up to look at a situation from other perspectives. How did you do? Did you realize that you had to stop looking at the extra $1,000,000 worth of ball bearings as a problem and begin to look at them as an opportunity. Not all opportunities are productive—(robot caviar???). But if all we focus on is the problem—which cannot be "solved," because we cannot send back the ball bearings—we will not get much further than finding and blaming the poor worker who goofed and over-ordered supplies.

If long-established membership declines, new growth, new worship settings, new music, new structural demands, the need to witness to a new world that is often neither interested nor attentive are not problems, then are they an opportunity? A calling? Our cross to bear? The new exile?

Call them what you will. But the critical question is, Where is the hand of God in this challenging environment that faces so many of our congregations? The question that needs to be answered by leaders of congregations is, Are the difficulties and dilemmas congregations have been facing in recent decades bad news and an "affront" to God? Or is the hand of God creating something new out of the old?

Lesson from the Exile

With remarkable insight and scholarship Walter Brueggemann points to the time of the exile and the writings of Jeremiah, Ezekiel, and Second Isaiah as similar to and therefore instructive for our own time. Pointing to the time of the destruction of the temple in Jerusalem and the captivity of the Israelites, Brueggeman sees the year 587 B.C.E. as the pivotal point in the Old Testament, marking the shift between what God did of old and what God was doing anew in the present.

> In understanding this literature, the date and events of 587 B.C.E. are decisive. The year 587 is the occasion when the temple in Jerusalem was burned, the holy city was destroyed, the davidic dynasty was terminated, the leading citizens deported. Public life in Judah came to an end. Our interest, however, is not in the descriptive character of a historical event. Rather our study is organized around "587" now treated as metaphor. We will refer to that date as a way of speaking about the end of any known world, about the dismantling of any system of meaning and power. By breaking the reference loose from its "facticity," the literature around 587 becomes available for analogous situations. The experience of ending and dismantlement may be charted in this way:

> The end of the   The reception of a
> known world and its   587 <   new world given by God
> relinquishment.   through these poets.

Judah had two tasks in this crisis of life and faith. It had to let go of the old world of king and temple that God had now taken from it. It had to receive from God's hand a new world which it did not believe was possible and which it would not have preferred or chosen.[6]

By moving from a reading of the events of 587 as historic fact to a reading as metaphor, Brueggeman clearly states that what was evidenced in this Old Testament experience of God is instructive for the present.

> My argument is that the loss of the authority of the dynasty and temple in Jerusalem is analogous to the loss of certainty, dominance, and legitimacy in our own time. In both cases the relinquishment is heavy and costly.[7]

And so, a prophetic poet like Jeremiah can offer lessons in leadership for today's leaders because he was able to see the rise and the expansion of the Babylonian empire and its substantial threat to Jerusalem not just as the turning of the political fortunes of his day but as the hand of God laying judgment against the city of Jerusalem and introducing change that a reluctant Israel would not choose for itself. Jeremiah reported: "Then the Lord said to me: Out of the north disaster shall break out on all the inhabitants of the land. For now I am calling the tribes of the kingdoms of the north, says the Lord; and they shall come and all of them shall set their thrones at the entrance of the gates of Jerusalem, against all its surrounding walls and against all the cities of Judah" (Jeremiah 1:14-16). Jeremiah was announcing that it may have seemed to the people of Judah that Babylonian greed and aggression were changing them, but the change was really the hand of God ("For now *I* am calling the tribes of the kingdoms of the north, *says the Lord*....").

This was certainly not a popular pronouncement. Jeremiah's leadership was not easily received by his contemporaries. But Jeremiah was able to stand as a leader and tell the people that this invasion and captivity was not just another problem to be solved by the next warrior problem-solver who could stand against the Babylonians. This was a time of large changes in assumptions and understanding, a time when people would need to relinquish what was old and known, and prepare themselves for the new that God was doing in their time.

We too need to exercise theological discernment as leaders of congregations. Problem to be solved? Or movement of God's spirit doing something new, which carries us in ways we had not considered?

Deciding What Type of Situation We Are Facing

If we assume our congregations are besieged by problems, then the appropriate response of leaders is to solve them. If it is broken, then fix it. But if we assume God is doing something new and different in this time of change, then leaders need to do something different, something other than seeking solutions and providing for the happiness and satisfaction of congregational members. As Brueggeman noted:

> The governing metaphor for this literature [Jeremiah, Ezekiel, and Second Isaiah] is that of exile. In this brief definitive period in Old Testament faith, pastoral responsibility was to help people enter into exile, to be in exile, and depart out of exile.[8]

If the questions facing our congregations are not just problems, then perhaps they are transforming moments. And transforming moments call for quite different leadership roles and understandings. Leaders do not just need to make things right. Theirs is the far more difficult role of introducing people to the new condition and helping them to learn new ideas, behaviors, and alternatives that are more appropriate to the new condition.

Leaders need to be able to determine the kind of a situation they are facing in order to determine their appropriate role and response, and this is new and unfamiliar work to most congregational leaders.

A remarkably helpful resource is found in Ronald Heifetz's reporting of the Leadership Education Project at the John F. Kennedy School of Government at Harvard University.[9] As well as being director of the Leadership Education Project, Heifetz is also a psychiatrist and a musician. He takes an interdisciplinary approach to leadership, and his facility with different models, modes, and assumptions helps him communicate new learnings. By crossing old disciplinary "fences," he gains and communicates new insights. Indeed, he seems to provide supportive evidence of a "Jeremiah moment" for congregations, who are invited to look across old sacred, theological, denominational, or traditional fences to see what new thing God is doing.

In the report Heifetz differentiates between three different kinds of situations leaders face.

Situation	Problem Definition	Solution & Implementation	Primary Locus of Responsibility	Kind of Work	Leadership Role	Example
Type I Technical Situation	Clear	Clear	Physician	Technical	Doctor has the expertise and the responsibility; patient depends upon doctor's knowledge, doctor depends upon patient's trust.	Broken bone; administration of antibiotic
Type II Technical/ Adaptive Situation	Clear	Requires Learning	Physician and Patient	Technical and Adaptive	Doctor may have a solution in mind but cannot implement it. The patient must learn and implement new behavior to effect a cure.	Stress to be treated with diet, exercise, and workload limits.
Type III Adaptive Situation	Requires Learning	Requires Learning	Patient more than Physician	Adaptive	Doctor must induce learning (both for doctor and patient) in order to define both the problem and the solution.	Terminal cancer in which the cancer is the "condition" and not the problem. The primary problem is the patient's adaption to a harsh reality.

Technical Situations

The first type of situation requires *technical* work: A *problem can be clearly defined* and a *solution can be clearly applied*. Heifetz, who has a medical background, uses the example of a broken bone. It is a clearly defined problem to which the physician has a clearly available solution. In a technical situation, the patient simply goes to the physician who has the solution and offers trust that the problem will be cared for.

In an earlier time, when congregations and their members and behaviors were similar to one another, primary leadership responsibilities were to stabilize and provide for the smooth operation of congregations. Many, if not most, of the situations leaders faced were technical. For example, if the problem was raising the necessary dollars to meet the coming year's proposed budget, then the technical response was to implement a program of tithing, pledged offering, or membership fees and communicate the need to members. Clear problem. Clear solution.

In the second and third types of situations Heifetz identified, however, leaders increasingly find that technical responses are not sufficient. *In other than technical situations, someone needs to learn something new in order to deal with the situation.*

Technical/Adaptive Situations

In the second situation, the *technical/adaptive* type, the *problem can be clearly defined* but the *solution requires learning*. Again using the medical model, Heifetz offers stress as an example. The problem is clear and well known. Medical science understands well the cause and the supporting behaviors that lead to unhealthy stress in an individual. To that extent stress appears to be a technical problem. But for the patient who is suffering from unhealthy stress, new learnings (adaptive behavior) must be found and practiced in order to respond to the situation. The patient must learn new dietary habits, new exercise behaviors, and new meditative or spiritual disciplines. Without the learning/adaptive behavior of the patient, the technical knowledge of medical science will do nothing to address the situation.

Adaptive Situations

In the third type of situation now facing leaders, a purely *adaptive* situation, *both the problem and the solution are unclear* and *new learning is required by all involved*. The medical example Heifetz offers is terminal cancer. Once cancer has been diagnosed as terminal, it ceases to be a problem that doctor and patient seek to cure. It becomes the condition under which the patient will live out the final chapter of his or her life. In this totally adaptive situation, the problem is not clear and there are no clear answers, and doctor and patient both must seek new learnings.

Indeed, in adaptive situations the doctor and patient even have to define the problem(s) in order to respond. The patient then needs to learn how to bring his or her life to an end. How will relationships be dealt with? How will assets be managed? How will bodily changes be accommodated? What spiritual resources and opportunities will be available?

Similarly, the doctor needs to learn about the patient. What spiritual and emotional resources does this person have? What family and relational support is available to this person? How much information can be shared by the doctor, and how quickly, without overwhelming the patient?

Adaptive Situations in Congregations

In a totally adaptive situation, the effectiveness of the response is dependent on the willingness of all parties to learn and to be open to changing behavior based on new learnings. For example, the simple technical situation that requires the development and support of next year's annual budget, referred to above, becomes much more of an adaptive situation in congregations where membership has become more diverse.

Consider the increasingly common experience of congregations in which 40 or 50 percent of the members have been active in the congregation for twenty years or more. These members are well versed in the traditions of the congregation, familiar with the theology and polity of their faith tradition, and practiced in regular financial giving as an act of faith that is usually a part of worship. To this group of people, stewardship, pledging, tithing, and a faith practice that includes some level of sacrificial giving makes perfect sense.

In a growing number of congregations, however, 25 to 35 percent of the members are new to the congregation and have been active for five years or less. Many of these people have come to the congregation seeking to meet clearly identified needs or to achieve specific goals in their lives or for their families. Increasingly these new members do not come with an awareness of the history, traditions, or practices of the faith tradition of the congregation they are joining. For many of these people, their entry into this congregation may be their first venture into a faith community. They come, not with the knowledge and expectations of the long-tenured members, but with the lessons and behaviors learned in a consumer society. They know what they are seeking. And, if they do not find it in this congregation, they will easily move on to look for it in another. Ideas such as stewardship, pledging, and tithing are often unusual and perhaps uncomfortable to them. They may not understand or respond to these ideas and traditions. They do, however, understand very well the need to pay for something of value received and they are very willing and anxious to pay their part to support the expenses and mission in a congregation where their needs are being met. So they write a check at the beginning or the end of the month when other bills are being paid, perhaps mailing it in and simply sitting quietly when the offering plate is passed in worship—all practices highly curious and sometimes offensive to the long-tenured members who faithfully place their gifts on the altar and accompany those gifts with prayers.

Congregational leaders practiced only in technical approaches will look at this as a technical problem and search for answers—technical solutions. They will ask: What kind of stewardship campaign do we need to get new members to respond like long-tenured members? How do we educate new members coming into the congregation through our membership classes, so they will behave like other members? In other words, if the assumption of the leaders is that they are facing problems that are interfering with the way things "should" happen in their congregation, they will seek to "fix" their stewardship approach or try to fix the "inappropriate" behavior of the newer members.

But if congregational leaders are willing to open themselves spiritually to the possibility that God is doing something new in their congregation, they will need to consider more adaptive approaches and ask very different questions such as: What is the meaning of membership in our congregation, and what beliefs, practices, and behaviors are expected from those who want to be a part of this community? How do we talk with one another in our congregation about material resources, given members' multiple expectations and the diversity of lifestyles? How do we teach the disciplines of our faith to people unfamiliar with them in ways they can understand and participate? To what extent do we understand our congregational budget to be about institutional expenses, and to what extent do we understand it as a spiritual discipline?

When congregational leaders were faced with mostly technical situations that could be viewed as problems, it was adequate to take a managerial posture and seek solutions to keep things running smoothly. Today leaders are increasingly confronted with adaptive situations that invite new learnings. Whatever situations they face, the critical difference in responses will not depend on how creative or thoughtful the leaders happen to be. The critical difference will be the assumptions and attitudes that will either make them seek quick-fix answers to frustrating problems or make them open, if not always anxious, to see what change the hand of God now offers.

Exercises for Leaders

1. Discuss the following questions:

- What changes have you faced as a congregation in the past ten years?
- Did your leaders view the changes as problems to be solved or fixed, or opportunities to be followed?
- In the situations that are currently facing you, do members hope you will find solutions that will "fix" things, or are they open and interested in learning new things about what God is doing?

2. On a piece of newsprint, divided as in the example below, list situations that currently face your congregation or leadership groups.

Technical	Technical/ Adaptive	Adaptive

For each technical/adaptive and each adaptive situation indicate:

- *Who* needs to learn something new?
- *What* do they need to learn or learn about?

CHAPTER 3

Beyond the Trees: Systems Theory as a Way to Look at Your Congregation

In a systems approach we look beyond the trees and see the forest.
—Peter Steinke, *Healthy Congregations*

The congregation was noted for its health and vitality and had committed itself to growth that would match its growing neighborhood. It appeared they had done everything necessary for growth. They had called a very able senior pastor, who had interest, experience, and a demonstrated track record in leading a growing congregation. They had developed a number of appropriate committees and work groups focused on invitation evangelism and membership care, and these groups were well resourced and had good leadership with solid staff support. The emphasis on growth was long term, and the congregation was well aware of the emphasis.

Yet the facts of the situation were surprising and, at first, disconcerting. Over a long period of time, the membership of the congregation never grew larger than 630, yet never seemed to sink below 580, in spite of the fact that the community around the congregation was growing with seemingly unlimited bounds. In fact, when the statistics were finally gathered for the previous twenty-year period, the leaders discovered that in twenty years they had gained 666 new members. And they had lost 666 members is the same period! Diabolical? No, not at all. It was simply a system seeking and finding its natural balance.

When the leaders of the congregation confronted the reality of their growth record, they began by trying to figure out what was "wrong." Like all volunteer organizations, they could easily point to things they could have done, as well as things they could have done better or differently. It was not until the senior pastor and a few key leaders began to talk about what it was like to work for growth in this congregation that the real dynamics began to be uncovered and understood.

The leaders described how they would begin to feel concerned and anxious as they became aware that membership was slipping toward the 580 mark. The anxiety caused by monthly membership reports and empty pews, which would produce comments from members at the close of worship, would spur them into action. Staff and committees would "put their shoulder to the wheel" and increase their activity level. Long-time members already in the pews would begin to look for visitors and go out of their way to talk with them. Visitors would begin to join, attendance figures would go up, and the pews would begin to refill. Membership would again begin to approach 630.

A natural byproduct of the increased efforts was the leaders' and committee members' satisfaction at seeing their efforts rewarded. But an unrecognized result of the increased satisfaction about recent membership gains was a release from the worry and the extra effort needed to make growth happen. Staff and committees typically felt tired from their efforts. When the pews were refilled, monthly reports were positive, and concerned comments about empty pews at worship ceased, it was natural for staff and committees to take time to regroup from their worry and work. Their attention to visitors and follow-up would begin to slack off. Long-time members would no longer express concern about empty pews, so they were not driven to look for visitors in their midst and began to look for old friends to visit with after worship, passing new faces with a quick hello in their search for old friends. This mode of relaxed operation would continue until the reports again began to indicate membership was slipping toward the 580 mark, comments were heard again about empty pews in worship, and the mounting anxiety and worry over membership would again spur staff and committees into action.

Was someone to blame? No. Were they doing something wrong? No. They were simply behaving like a system that had found its natural balance between 580 and 630 members. It was not until staff and members understood the natural limits of their system that they were able to change the appropriate parts of the system to allow the growth they felt called to seek.

We need new ways to look at and understand our congregations. It is not that our old ways are wrong. It is more that our old and familiar ways of looking and understanding can be limited and limiting.

As I suggested in chapter 2, the way we understand the situations our congregations face is a spiritual issue. Our understanding and our response to congregational life have much to do with our spiritual assumptions and attitudes. If we believe the current situation in our congregation is an affront to God, then we will seek to "fix" what went wrong. But if we believe we should be open to transformational change that may well reveal the hand of God in our midst, we will stop trying to fix things and we will begin to try to figure out how to ride the wave God seems to be sending our way.

A Conceptual Issue

But this is not only a spiritual issue. It is a conceptual issue as well. We need to pay attention to the ideas and the language we use when we work with our congregations, for ideas and the way we use language are extremely powerful tools. Ideas and language provide a focus and framework for our understanding. They also prevent us from seeing beyond that same focus and framework. The power of ideas and of language to help us to understand or to limit our understanding should not be underestimated.

One of my favorite stories from an anthropology course in college demonstrates the point well. A South Sea Islands people built their huts out of materials they found on their islands. They used "stonewood" to build the hearth to hold the fire they used for cooking and warmth. Stonewood was by far the hardest wood to be found in their forests. Yet because it was wood, it would eventually catch fire and frequently— usually every two or three years—the family's hut burned down. The response of the community was swift and sure. People would interrupt their usual activities and lend their hand in rebuilding the lost hut. And when it came to rebuilding the hearth in the new hut they would use— yes, stonewood. Inevitably the rebuilt hut would burn down again. A good portion of community life was spent rebuilding each other's huts.

Although these people were of a simpler, less developed culture, we need to be clear that they were not unintelligent. Yet despite their experience that huts burned down regularly from fires originating in the hearth, and despite the fact that they knew stonewood came from living trees, they continued to use flammable material to house their fires. Why? One of the lasting lessons of undergraduate anthropology was the power of language and the images it suggests. Despite their experience, the name "*stone*wood" suggested to these people that they were building their hearth using material so hard it would behave as stone. Did they not learn from experience as hut after hut burned down? Surprisingly the answer seems to be no.

Language and the assumptions carried by the images we use are surprisingly powerful and surprisingly limiting, because they define the way in which we will think about our world. We cannot assume that our own culture, which we might look at as more developed or more sophisticated than others, is any less focused, controlled, or limited by the language, images, and ideas we use to understand it.

General Systems Theory

For several centuries our culture, with its Western European beginnings, has looked at the structure of experience using a mechanistic worldview. According to this view, the world is much like a *machine* made of component parts all working together in synchronized fashion to some purposeful end. To understand that world and one's place and purpose in it, break the larger machine into its component parts and seek to understand the individual parts and how they work together. This mechanistic worldview is powerful. It rests at the heart of our sciences, which have dissected animal, vegetable, and mineral bodies into their component parts so that we enjoy medical, pharmacological, and environmental sciences of truly amazing depth. It rests at the heart of our government, which can be reduced to the component parts: the executive, legislative, and judicial branches. Similarly, corporations are reduced to their executive, management, and production levels, with staff and line functions understood to have clear and distinct responsibilities. Parts are organized into larger functioning bureaucracies that in turn control the whole organization or organism by understanding and managing the lesser component parts. This model is sometimes called reductionistic dualism: Larger complicated systems are reduced to their component parts so they can be understood and controlled. The model draws dualistic comparisons (something is "either this or that") between the parts in an effort to determine their place and function in the whole. This worldview allows us to understand our world and its component parts so well that it has, in fact, provided a means to get us to the Moon and Mars and into subatomic worlds once never known.

But a mechanistic world view limits as well. It assumes that life is made of component parts that can be named, understood, and controlled, and based on this view we begin to respond to life mechanistically. We have discussed above, for example, the automatic and natural response of leaders who want to quickly "fix" their congregation when things do not go smoothly. Fixing is what we do to machines. A cardiac surgeon tries to fix an ill or a failing heart. But a parent or a spouse finds mechanism of limited usefulness when dealing with a broken heart. Mechanism does have its limits.

There are other ways, different languages, and less mechanistic ideas that we can use to help us to understand and to respond to our congregations more appropriately. Systems theory provides a helpful, more organic language and ideas that give rise to more appropriate responses, responses beyond solving problems and seeking control. If our language and assumptions are mechanistic, the responsibility of leaders must surely be to fix things when they are broken and to be in control of the results or product. But if our language and ideas are more organic and systemic, the responsibility of the leader may more appropriately be focused on nourishing and nurturing the system, not fixing it. Rather than seeking control, leaders at times need to know simply how to respond appropriately to the needs of their system to allow it to do what it is designed to do.

Recently, my family was reintroduced to a familiar example of the difference between mechanism and systems-thinking when our friends' daughter had a baby, Jillian. Jillian is a marvelous little baby, a complete and wonderful little "system" all by herself. She is a beautiful child with a wonderful smile and is easily the center of attraction at any gathering in her new home. She is seemingly perfect.

But she cries.

Enough years have passed since our own children were babies that I have clearly lost touch with how to respond, and I am simply left to wonder how her mother, grandmother, and my wife (when she is lucky enough to be asked to baby-sit) know what to do when Jillian cries. In my more "mechanistic moods," my response is to want to "fix" Jillian by controlling whatever is bothering her. In their much more organic, systemic response, the women in Jillian's life listen to her cry in order to understand and provide what she naturally needs. And they say things like, "Oh, that's a hungry cry," or, "Listen to her; that's a wet cry. She needs to be changed."

Based on our mechanical worldview of leadership, we often want to control and to fix. A systems theory view of leadership offers tools and language to observe, understand, and respond appropriately to the natural needs of the system we are leading.

Systems theory invites us to look at our congregations, not in their component parts, but as a whole. Systems theory itself is not a fully integrated "theory," as we might think of a number of other research-based scientific or social scientific theories. Beginning with the work and writings of people like Ludwig von Bertalanffy, Abraham Maslow, and Arthur Koestler, what is referred to as "general systems theory" is, in fact, a modern scientific philosophy.[1] It is a way of looking at our world through the lens of a new language developed out of our experience and thoughtful inquiries into that experience.

We are not working here with a popular outgrowth of general systems theory often referred to as "family systems theory." Family systems theory is an insightful way to understand and respond to the emotional and relational life within families and has been helpfully and appropriately applied to congregations by people such as Edwin Friedman and Peter Steinke.[2] Rather, my interest is in helping leaders become familiar with a language and a lens that allow them to see broader general patterns that go beyond the congregation's emotional or relational life. A general systems approach allows leaders to understand congregations by looking through the lens of certain key ideas to see and to understand how to respond to the whole congregation. Such an approach does not invite leaders to control the congregation. Rather, leaders can take a much more organic approach to understanding their congregation and determining an appropriate response that would enable the congregation to do what it naturally and faithfully is able to do in a time of change.

Central Characteristics of General Systems

Several characteristics of general systems are exceptionally helpful to congregational leaders. These characteristics allow us to view our congregations as organisms rather than machines. An "organism" is something with "diverse organs and parts that function together as a whole to maintain life and its activities."[3] When we view a congregation as an organism, we try to understand how things come together to give it life rather than taking them apart to see what might be broken. We want to view the congregation as an organism:

- with interrelated and interconnected parts
- whose behavior is less causal than connected
- that naturally seeks balance or equilibrium, and
- in which the parts and the whole interact.

This new language may seem confusing and the opportunities it offers to understand and lead our congregations may be unclear. But let's take a closer look at each of these key systems characteristics and link them to leadership in congregations.

Interrelated and Interconnected Parts

The older mechanistic worldview invites us to move from a description of the *whole* to component *parts*. Go to a doctor with a general complaint, and she will look at your parts: your circulatory system, your immune system, your skeletal system, and so forth, to find out where the problem is, and then she will go into that system to find out which part is the problem. The whole person is approached in terms of what is wrong with one or more of his or her parts. Similarly, when you take your automobile into the shop for work, the mechanic determines which system is ailing and then goes into that system to correct the necessary part.

　　General systems theory invites us not to go from the whole to its component parts but to begin with the parts in order to understand the whole. In this case the doctor would explore diet, exercise, age, and other related characteristics and behaviors of the patient in order to respond to the symptoms in the skeletal or circulatory parts of the system.

Rather than looking at the forest (the whole) in order to understand the trees (the parts), we look at the connections between the trees (the parts) in order to understand and respond to the forest (the whole.) In fact, the notion of seeing or not seeing the forest for the trees is an apt image for wrestling with the interrelatedness and interconnectedness of systems like congregations.

When speaking about three images that have changed her life and her understanding of organizations, Margaret Wheatley offers the example of the interconnectedness of aspen trees. She writes:

> I recently learned from my son's fifth grade teacher that the largest known living organism on the planet lives in Utah, where we now live. My son got excited and thought it was Bigfoot, but it's not. It's a grove of aspen trees that covers thousands of acres. When we look at them we think, "Oh, look at all the trees." When botanists looked underground they said, "Oh, look at this system, it's all one. This is one organism." You see, when aspen trees propagate, they don't send out seeds or cones, they send out runners, and a runner runs for the light (there's wonderful imagery in all of this), and we say, "Aha! There's another tree…" until we look underground, and we see that it is all one vast connection.[4]

There are other examples in nature that tell us of this interrelatedness and connection between what seem to be independent parts. Research pathologist and former president of the Sloan-Kettering Cancer Center, Lewis Thomas, suggests that the sixth of the seven wonders of the modern world is the termite, which offers a prime example of interconnectedness and collectivity. Writes Thomas:

> There is nothing at all wonderful about a single, solitary termite, indeed there is really no such creature, functionally speaking, as a lone termite, any more than we can imagine a genuinely solitary human being; no such thing. Two or three termites gathered together on a dish are not much better; they may move about and touch each other nervously, but nothing happens. But keep adding more termites until they reach a critical mass, and then the miracle begins. As though they had suddenly received a piece of extraordinary news, they organize in platoons and begin stacking up pellets to

precisely the right height, then turning the arches to connect the columns, constructing the cathedral and its chambers in which the colony will live out its life for the decades ahead, air-conditioned and humidity controlled, following the chemical blueprint coded in their genes, flawlessly, stone-blind. They are not the dense mass of individual insects they appear to be; they are an organism, a thoughtful, meditative brain on a million legs.[5]

What is suggested in these examples from nature is that there is something organic about systems, which are not at all mechanical or reducible to interchangeable parts. The very nature of a system is that it cannot be understood or appreciated by looking only at one or more parts (trees or termites). Instead, we use the information from the parts to learn about the whole (forest or mound).

In one of my favorite experiments in animal behavior, also described in the writings of Lewis Thomas, we get a clearer hint of how the whole supersedes its various parts. Thomas describes an experiment with bees, which are considered by scientists to be rather unintelligent insects. Biologists studying their behavior place a source of sugar close to the hive of bees, so that the bees can easily find the sugar and begin to learn the rules of the game they are about to play. Then, at regular intervals, the biologists move the dish of sugar progressively farther and farther away from the hive in increments of about 25 percent at each move. Soon the sugar target is moving at rather large increments of hundreds of feet at each change. Thomas writes, "Sooner or later, while this process is going on, the biologist shifting the dish of sugar will find his bees are out there waiting for him, precisely where the next position had been planned."[6]

It is rather unsettling to think about bees having some form of consciousness that is able to figure out a rather complicated "game" and even predict its next steps. But even more unsettling (or insightful?) is the notion that perhaps it is not the individual bee or bees (the parts) that have such intelligence. Rather, this experiment suggests that the actual organism that has the intelligence to figure the game out is the hive (the whole). To consider only the individual bee and not its interrelationship to the hive would be to misunderstand the full organism of the hive, which is highly intelligent. There are a multitude of examples in the animal sciences where the whole—the hive, colony, or group—demonstrates a consciousness or wisdom that goes beyond the capability or intelligence of any one individual animal in the collective. Somehow in the interconnectedness and interrelatedness of the parts, the whole is endowed with or establishes a presence and capability that is well beyond the simple sum of its parts.

One of the clearest implications of this fact in the life of a congregation is that the presenting "problem" being experienced is not what needs to be "fixed" but provides a way of understanding what is going on in the larger life of the congregation.

Typically, for example, leaders will want to talk to me about the problem of not meeting their budget. The more mechanistic approach that seeks to understand the parts from the whole (using reductionist language and ideas) would suggest that we take a look at the stewardship or membership drive that has been used to invite people to support the budget. Did we have the right program? Use the right communication tools and opportunities? Describe our need so that people understood how many bills we have to pay? Ask people to give at the most opportune time of the year? And so on. We move from the larger problem of the budget to the smaller, component parts: how we get people to support the budget. This approach produces a very familiar problem-solving strategy.

But a systems approach would suggest that leaders look at more than a presenting problem to understand the relationships and connections in the congregation. We ask about the whole congregation and wonder what is going on in the whole that is creating this discomfort in the budgetary part of the congregation's life. Is there a lack of energy in the congregation? Why are people not excited about financially supporting the ministry that is an expression of their faith? Are the programs and ministry of the church unfocused, so that people do not see the connection with their faith? Do the goals and the programs of the church speak to only a small group of people in the church, and other people do not think the congregation is important to them and do not see themselves benefiting or participating? In fact, financial giving, like average attendance at worship, tends to be a rather clear systemic signal of what is going on within the whole congregation. This symptomatic characteristic suggests that problems with or changes in finances and attendance at worship are often, or usually, not problems in and of themselves but reflect other issues in the life of the congregation.

Leaders' mechanistic response would be to identify the problem and work to solve it. If we are short of funds, perhaps we need a second fund drive before the end of the year, or perhaps we need to improve our pledge drive letters, or perhaps we need to ask two or three of the wealthier members to do a little rescuing this year by giving some extra money to fill in the gap.

The mechanistic approach to leadership is very familiar. One relatively large congregation in a small city was faced with a substantial budget shortfall for the third year in a row, and the response of the leadership was to spend an inordinate amount of time going over expenses and trying to make up the difference by reducing the number and cost of mailings sent to members (including quarterly giving statements that might encourage updated giving!), cutting back on office and cleaning supplies, and making rules about turning out lights when you left a room. The mechanistic response—finding a problem and solving it by controlling its smaller component parts (or in this case the smaller component expenses)—can miss the larger and more significant picture to which the budget shortfall is connected.

A systems approach that recognizes the interconnectedness of the parts of the life of the congregation understands that the support of the budget is connected to members' appreciation of and participation in the goals and focus of their congregation's ministry, their sense of whether their needs are being met, and their sense of being included and listened to. Assuming that (and checking to be sure that) the budgetary problems are not tied to fiscal mismanagement, leaders using a systems approach would wonder what information is to be found in the congregation's lack — of support of the budget and ask how leaders can appropriately respond to the *congregation's* needs, not the *budget's* need.

Less Causal Than Connected Behavior

The second characteristic of general systems suggests that it is not particularly helpful to try to find the *cause* of a problem. The idea that a cause rests at the heart of a problem or situation is born from our long experience with mechanistic thinking. This causal thinking is based on the concept that every effect experienced in the congregation can be attributed to a cause that must be either appreciated or changed.

It has been estimated, however, that of the variables that currently impact the life of a congregation, only 40 to 50 percent are under the control of the congregation itself. Changing cultural values and lifestyles of the larger population, people moving into or away from the area served by a congregation, traffic patterns or highway systems shifting away from the congregation's site, changing behavioral lifestyles that allow much less time for congregationally focused volunteer activities, a pervasive fear of crime that minimizes the amount of travel people are willing to do in the evenings, are all examples of significant changes that congregations cannot control but that impact the ongoing life of the congregation.

Obviously, many things affect what is happening in our congregations. But the linear assumption that each effect has a cause (A ⇨ B) invites us to believe that we can control whatever is happening. Many congregations search for *the* cause by asking "what" is wrong. Unable to come up with an answer to that question in the current complex environment, congregations then often reframe the question: "Who" is wrong? If people cannot find the *cause*, they will try to find someone to *blame*.

General systems theory offers a more accurate description of our situation by recognizing that the variables that influence are less about causes and more about connections. Rather than searching for the "A" that "causes" ⇨ "B" it is more accurate and helpful to become aware of all the variables that influence the current situation. So a much more realistic description of a ministry setting, for example, looks more like this:

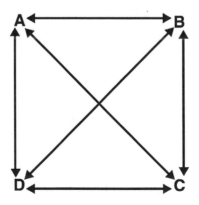

The role and responsibility of leaders in this setting is not to fix whatever is causing the problem but to describe and understand what various issues or variables they will need to address in order to lead the system.

An example of a more systemic approach can be found in the work of Roy Oswald and Speed Leas concerning new member assimilation.[7] After identifying a number of significant church growth factors that are outside of the control of the congregation, they then list five variables that are within the control of leaders:

- A positive identity
- Congregational harmony and cooperation
- The pastor's ability to generate enthusiasm
- Involvement in social action or social service
- Programming

Being able to approach the congregation as a system and identify the variables or factors that influence what is happening offers helpful alternatives for leaders that the more mechanistic and solution-oriented approach misses.

Systems theory allows leaders to understand that a number of inter-related issues will need to be addressed simultaneously in order to accomplish change, because the variables influencing the situation are connected. For example, using the research of Oswald and Leas, it is fairly easy to see connections between a positive identity in the congregation and congregational harmony. A positive identity is attractive to people, who can clearly understand what a congregation has committed itself to and how it may address a spiritual or social need they themselves feel. So if a congregation has committed itself to effective work with youth and young families, people seeking such ministry will know they may find a home here. If in the midst of their excellenct work with youth and young families, however, there is a fairly high level of discord among decision makers in the congregation, people will sense it easily. The experience is like going to visit close friends for dinner and realizing five minutes after you arrived that they were having an argument before you showed up. No one is saying anything about the argument, but everybody knows they were having it. The environment is not welcoming and inviting.

Disharmony, in the context of our discussion here, functions as a passive barrier. Lack of harmony, discord in the congregation, is a barrier to new people, and it will keep them out. Harmony by itself does nothing to invite people in, however. Achieving congregational harmony and learning how to manage differences and make decisions does not offer the clarity that comes from a positive identity that suggests to people that they should become connected with this particular congregation.

The way other variables Oswald and Leas have identified are related to systems thinking can be explored in similar fashion to demonstrate that an effective approach to becoming a growing and inviting congregation takes leaders into a number of different areas in the life of their congregation. Growth is not a matter of finding and fixing a cause to a problem, or finding a magic program or person who alone will achieve the goal of the ministry.

The strength of a systems approach, which recognizes and honors the connectedness of issues or variables, is that it allows leaders to ask the essential question about what areas or factors will need to be addressed to achieve the goals that have been set for ministry. The areas or factors are multiple and connected and will need to be addressed together. The more mechanistic causal approach will commonly lead a congregation to sink a significant level of member, staff, and financial resources into a "program" for growth, only to discover that what worked so well and was so highly praised in another congregation seems to have little or no effect in their congregation. Or a frustrated congregation will change its clergy, convinced that they had identified "who" the problem is, only to realize two years later that a new pastor has not changed the congregational system as much as the congregational system has changed the new clergy leader to behave in the old ways they were trying to fix. Such causal approaches to leadership do not serve congregational systems well, because they do not attend to the connectedness of the factors influencing their setting.

Naturally Seeking Balance or Equilibrium

The third characteristic of a system is that all systems seek a balance that is usually experienced by leaders as resistance to change. Decision makers have been described as people in systems from whom leadership

is simultaneously expected and resisted as a matter of course.[8] The fact
that leadership is met with resistance is not necessarily a problem. It
does not mean that people are diabolical and mean-spirited when they
do not easily and naturally conform to the directions offered by their
leaders. Yet it is often the case that when resistance is experienced,
leaders increase their efforts to persuade and push for change as if the
resistance is inappropriate.

A Game

Invite people in your group to stand facing each other in pairs,
with their arms outstretched and touching one another lightly at
the palms. Offer the following role descriptions.

1. The taller person in the pair (following our cultural myth that
leaders are tall) is your congregation's newly arrived
clergyperson, who is very glad to be here because he or she
sees the rich potential in the congregation and cannot wait to
get started. As a matter of fact, the clergyperson is somewhat
puzzled that other leaders who have been here longer have not
seen the exciting possibilities and begun working on them long
ago.

2. The shorter person in the pair is a layperson who has been a
member of this congregation for thirty years and has been on
the governing board for twenty-seven years. She or he is very
glad the new clergyperson has arrived and is anxious to begin
working with this new leader. This long-tenured layperson also
"knows how things are done here."

   Once everyone is clear about their role, offer the following in-
structions:

   A. This is a nonverbal exercise. Without talking, I would like
   the new clergy leader to express with his or her hands the
   potential in this congregation and the direction in which the

(continued on next page)

(continued)

congregation should go. (It is common at this point in the exercise for laughter to break out as the clergy are naturally met with resistance by the hands of the board member.)

B. Clergy, you seem to be meeting resistance. Perhaps this is because you have not made yourselves clear. Clergy, please use your hands to express yourself more clearly, so the board member will understand.

(You might want to stop the exercise soon after this second direction, because people typically begin laughing even more as they dig in for a real wrestling match!)

Systems naturally and characteristically seek a balance, an equilibrium. If you push a system toward change, it naturally pushes back. If you push it harder, it pushes back harder in order to maintain its balance. If that is true of systems in general, it is particularly true of congregations, which maintain at least part of their identity through a history and tradition that many people feel must be preserved.

The drive for balance is also seen in the polarity between management and leadership I spoke of in chapter 1. Managers are responsible for stability and making sure daily operations go smoothly. Leaders are responsible for leading change and making sure ministry is taking place in the appropriate arenas. Managers make it tough for leaders to initiate change. Leaders make it difficult for managers to maintain stability. Both managers and leaders are equally vital to the life and health of the congregation. But as one pushes, the other naturally resists. Any destabilized system will first respond by seeking a new stability.

The most helpful image I have found to visualize this natural response is a mobile: a hanging work of art whose component pieces seem to be free-floating in space, though the wires and braces keep them interconnected and interrelated. Changing or removing just one part of the mobile causes the rest of the system to swing and sway as it adapts to the change. And the immediate need and response of the mobile is to find and reestablish a stability that allows it to maintain its parts in as close to the original positions as it can manage, given the changes introduced.

Too often and too quickly this natural dynamic of systems is evaluated negatively, and the relationship between leaders and members in the congregation becomes adversarial as people sense opposition instead of balance. The natural need for a balance between change and stability within the congregational system often breaks down into mistrust: Members think leaders are destroying the stability they have come to depend upon, and leaders think members are undermining their efforts to move into a changing future. Clergy and key lay leaders often feel betrayed when they are invited to be "visionary leaders" but then are actively resisted when they speak of the vision.

With some clear sensitivity to the characteristics of its system, one mid-size urban congregation approached a critical phase in its planning. They obviously would need to make some changes. The pastor and planning team saw that they needed to be more extroverted in their community so others would know that they were there and would feel welcome in the congregation. They also needed to make their worship service, which was of excellent quality but very traditional character, more inviting to people who were not well versed in the tradition. And they also needed to open up their leadership circle to include newer voices in the decision-making seats to help design some of the changes they would have to go through. As the pastor described these needed changes that were identified as a result of their planning process, most of the members understood them—rationally. But emotionally there were any number of reactions the planners had to deal with, including charges that they were "throwing the baby out with the bath water" when they spoke of changing worship, being irresponsible by inviting very new members to make decisions for a congregation they did not understand yet, and so on.

From a mechanistic worldview, if the congregational "machine" does not respond well, leaders are responsible for making it work, so leaders intensify their efforts at change, becoming more persuasive and more directive. But the natural response of a system seeking balance typically is to increase its resistance to increased pressure to change, leading to the we/they division between leaders and members that is so characteristic of times of change.

The alternative that the systems theory worldview offers is the acknowledgment that reasonable resistance to change is typical and characteristic of healthy systems, and that there is information for leaders in resistance. In fact, by listening to voices of resistance, leaders are offered a description of concerns and issues that need to be considered and included (not necessarily fixed) to help the congregation change. The importance of listening to this resistance will be addressed in a later chapter.

In this case the leaders did listen. At a weekend retreat for the congregation in which the learnings of the planning team were being shared, some members of the congregation talked about feeling like their security was being threatened and their fear that they would "have no rock to stand on." The image of a secure rock to stand on is powerful and speaks of a natural stability needed even in the midst of change. Rather than fight this resistance, the planning leaders invited it. Their response was to say, "Let's describe the rock." The agreement leaders made with members that weekend was that the "rock" of stability that would be necessary for their congregation to move securely into the future would be both described and honored by the leaders. But once there was agreement about the fundamental values and practices ("the rock") that were essential to preserve, leaders would be free to experiment in ways that would not destroy the rock. The image that everyone left the retreat with was of a "rock" upon which leaders would at all times keep one foot. If they did that, then members would be understanding and supportive as leaders "danced" about experimentally with the other foot to meet the changing needs of their new situation. This image provided a new balance for their time of change. From a systems perspective it is much better to learn from a natural resistance and to negotiate a creative but necessary balance than it is to fight resistance and seek to win.

The Interplay Between Parts and Whole

The final characteristic of congregations viewed through general systems theory can be captured in the term "holon," which is a word first coined by futurist Arthur Koestler to suggest that everything is always both a part and a whole simultaneously.[9] Imagine a chair standing in the middle of a room. Like all functional chairs, it is a whole. It has a seat, a back, four legs, and perhaps arm rests. It is a whole, complete within itself. But at the same time, it is a part. The room in which it is located would be incomplete without chairs for people to sit on. So the chair that is a whole unto itself is also a necessary part of the room if the room is to be whole.

We can take this mental image further, for the room is also a whole. It has everything necessary to be a complete and functioning whole— walls, a floor, a ceiling, windows, doors. By itself, with all its component parts in place, the room is a whole. The building in which the room is located, however, would be incomplete if it did not have this room. Although the room is complete and a whole by itself, it is also a part of the larger building, which is a whole.

Different *levels* exist in any system. Children love to play with levels, and TV programs such as "Sesame Street" provide excellent examples of moving visually from micro to macro levels as tiny worlds get expanded into related and connected giant worlds and vice versa. The connection that holon provides for leaders is the awareness that you can get information from any level in a congregational system and use it to help explain what is being experienced and what is needed on higher or lower levels. This interplay between parts and the whole explains why scientists concerned about global warming or continental pollution can make accurate predictions by monitoring small areas or observing only a few species of animals. The smaller area or species is capable of telling the larger story of what is happening on the global level.

From a systems worldview, this suggests that one of the effective ways leaders can understand and respond to the needs of the larger congregation is to be aware of the needs and feelings they are dealing with — or have dealt with themselves. The leader or leadership group in a congregation, which can be understood as a whole, is also a part of and connected to the larger whole of the congregation. One level of a system can inform the other levels of the same system. Expressing this a bit more technically, David Armstrong, an organizational psychologist with the Tavistock Institute, a research and consulting organization based in London, speaks of giving attention to the interpretation of emotional experience in the meeting between leader and organization. This emotional interchange between the smaller levels of the organization as experienced by the leader is a proper way of understanding the larger organizational system.[10] In other words, the way in which the larger system treats and relates to the leader carries information about the issues or concerns that belong to the larger system.

Essentially a systems approach can help us to understand that leaders will need to experience themselves what congregations experience in a time of change, and conversely congregations will have to learn and experience what leaders have learned and experienced in order to go through change. This can be seen rather clearly in planning. A governing board, seeing the need for planning, appoints a planning task force to look at the future and to do necessary visioning for the congregation. At this point the planning task force is a microcosm of the whole congregation. The task force is the principle of holon in action. It is a whole by itself, but it is still a part of the larger congregation at the same time.

In order to do its task, the planning task force is going to have to learn new things. So typically the task force will participate in activities that will change its experience in the congregation. Members will read books together, have structured conversations, share Bible study to help them focus, study demographic and psychographic data about their community, and interview congregational leaders and groups of members. Through all this work they are systematically drawing a bigger picture of the congregation in its community and its cultural context. As they work, their congregation begins to look different to them, because they change the way they look at it and they begin to understand the need for changes. Change makes sense to them and it is consistent with their new understanding and experience of their congregation.

At the same time, these planning task force members have their own feelings about their congregation. They have had time to think about, and to feel, the discomfort of changing their worship experience in order to be inviting to new people, and they may have experienced the shock or the upheaval of visiting a neighboring congregation whose worship style has changed "too much" and realizing that is not where their congregation is heading. Or they may have had time to consider what it means to step down as chairperson of a committee they have been on for twelve years in order to allow other members to work in that area of congregational life unhindered by past routines and traditions. They have had time to deal with their fears about what they might lose. They have had time to sort out their confusion about why the changes are necessary and how they can maintain their relationship to the congregation through the time of change.

The concept of holon suggests that the congregation will need to follow a path similar to the path their planning team has taken. The planning task force (the part) has experienced what the congregation (the whole) will also need to experience. The congregation will need to learn a lot of what the planning task force has learned, so they too can see the bigger picture that suggests necessary changes. The congregation will need time and opportunities for constructive and safe conversation to explore their feelings about what they might be losing and the confusion they are feeling as they hear about changes that they cannot quite visualize yet. Holon helps leaders to understand that if they can remember their own experience, their feelings and reactions, in the process of planning, they will be better able to help the congregation with its feelings and reactions.

Yet from a mechanistic worldview, planning teams typically do all the necessary work in isolation. They discern and prepare strategies to address necessary changes and simply summarize them in recommendations for the future that are delivered to the governing board for vote and approval. Usually such planning teams are surprised and offended by the resistance they receive from people who do not understand how they got to their conclusions and why "they are ruining our congregation!"

From a systems point of view of the holon, the planning team might recognize that as a task force they need to give the board members and congregational members new information in order for them to understand the context of the changes suggested. Or they may have to plan for opportunities and an adequate amount of time for board and congregational members to talk about and deal with their feelings about some changes before the planners rush ahead and ask for decisions.

The planning team will need to resist its own natural temptation to overcome the resistance of others by proving that they are right, and they will need to look at the information the board or the members are offering in their resistance. Does the resistance provide clues about what in the system is of value and should be preserved? Does the resistance suggest that people are simply locked into old unchallenged ideas? Or are they confused? The planning team will need to recall what they learned that helped them let go of their own old perceptions and find ways to help others follow a path the planning team has already covered. Does the resistance suggest that the people who have heard their recommendations are angry and frustrated about what they think they are losing in the change? The planning team will need to recall what they were feeling as they looked at changes facing their congregation and find ways to help board and congregational members to explore those feelings.

Once again, the power and the opportunity of a systems approach to leadership in a time of change is found in the way it allows leaders to remove themselves from the impossible task of trying to fix things and make everyone happy. Instead, leaders can use their own experience to respond to the congregation, knowing that what they themselves experienced when preparing for change interplays with the larger congregation. Systems theory provides a much more organic and faithful way to understand and engage the needs of the whole congregation and to nurture it through a dynamic change that is, in fact, rather natural albeit uncomfortable.

Looking at Your Congregation

Leaders must look at, understand, and then appropriately respond to the needs of their congregation in a time of change. Leadership is not about knowing where the congregation is supposed to end up and controlling it to be sure it gets there. In fact, leaders often have to describe what their congregations are experiencing or feeling in order to understand what is going on. And then, with appropriate responses, leaders need to nurture the natural gifts of the congregation and help provide new learnings in order to help it manage a time of change.

The next three chapters describe several lenses that can be used to diagnose where a congregation is in the midst of change and what leadership responses might be needed. These lenses will be approached from a systems perspective. You will be invited to ask different questions about your congregation and to assess where your congregation is located within the model of change being offered.

Chapter 4 will ask the questions: Where are we in the wilderness of change? What part of the journey do we need to give attention to?

Chapter 5 will ask the questions: Where are we emotionally as we experience change? What feelings do we need to address?

Chapter 6 will ask the questions: What is the appropriate way to talk about change? What are appropriate strategies for introducing our changes?

What Goes Round, Comes Round

Before we leave this chapter, it is worth noting that although we have been using the powerful language of systems theory that comes out of a scientific worldview (particularly, in this case, the human social sciences), we have not ventured too far from a spiritual understanding of congregations. In fact, we may have come closer to home than we suspect.

One of the startling discoveries of the new sciences, particularly quantum physics, is that the more one explores experience using the language of quantum physics, the closer one comes to the language of Eastern mystics such as that found in Tao Buddhism.[11] Both focus on wholeness, unity, and equilibrium. This suggests that where once science and religion were viewed as far different disciplines exploring far different realities, we are now coming full circle, allowing science to inform faith, and understanding science by looking through faith. The powerful ideas of scientific disciplines such as general systems theory are helping us to find the wholeness we have been seeking in faith communities.

This connection of disciplines and parts is where we started as people of faith. We have long understood that faith is expressed in wholeness. Consider the way 1 Corinthians 12 uses the image of the connections and interdependence of the parts of the body to express the wholeness to be found in Christ. ("For just as the body is one and has many members, and all the members of the body, though many, are one body, so it is with Christ." 1 Cor. 12:12)

Walter Wink points out that the Book of Revelation is unique in New Testament writings in that the seven letters to the seven churches that make up that book are all addressed to the *angels* of those churches,[12] where other letters in the New Testament were addressed to the *people* who made up the congregation. Wink recognizes that many people today may be uncomfortable with that idea. The essence of the angel of the church, however, is that the congregation, like a person, is unified and whole and has personality and identifying characteristics. Curiously we tend not to be bothered by the similar idea of "corporate culture," which suggests that a business or institution has personality characteristics that shape and determine its responses and relationships. For example, my wife and I quickly decided after a second visit to one doctor's office that we had not yet found the new doctor we were seeking.

We walked into the office and were greeted by the receptionist/nurse, who opened the sliding glass window to the reception area and asked (without greeting), "Do you still have the same insurance?" When we answered "yes," she slid the window closed, still without greeting or any other acknowledgment. The culture was clear. The "personality" of the place had been exposed, and we did not need much more evidence to convince us that we would be treated in this place as part of a health care "manufacturing plant" in which pieces of us, but not our whole person, would be addressed by the doctor.

Wink's biblical work helps us to see that the congregation has an angel, just as a corporation has a culture, an integrated "personality" that is expressed in its wholeness. In fact, Wink describes the inner spirit of the congregation as being composed of two voices, the voice of "personality," which reveals where the congregation came from and who and what was significant in bringing it to the present moment, and the voice of "vocation," which tells us where the congregation is going, what God calls the congregation to do in the future.

The responsibility of leaders is not to find the voice of vocation for the angel of the congregation and thus to win over the voice of personality, so the congregations can be controlled into the future. In fact, the experience at the Alban Institute is that pushing only the voice of vocation engenders disabling conflict, because only one part of the whole system is being addressed. Rather, Wink suggests that the responsibility of the faithful leader is to integrate the two voices of the angel, personality and vocation, so the congregation can move into the future using the strengths and gifts learned from the past (personality) without being so constrained by those strengths and gifts that the congregation is detached from and unresponsive to the future (vocation).[13]

The understanding of our congregations through the disciplines of the human sciences and theology offers a new wholeness once unavailable to leaders. Seeing our congregations as integrated and balanced organisms of past and future, personality and vocation, can free leaders from fruitless tasks of fixing and invite them to pick up more productive tasks of leading.

Exercises for Leaders

Play with the following charts to help shape conversation among leaders (or within yourself) using new approaches from a systems point of view. Do not worry about where the conversation takes you at the moment, and do not try to rush on to solutions or actions as a product of your conversation.

Begin by identifying one or more situations or issues leaders view as important to the future of your congregation. Be sure you are not talking about "technical" problems—clear problems with clear solutions. Look for "adaptive" situations instead.

A. A congregation is an organism with interrelated and interconnected parts.

What variables are connected to this situation?	Over which variables do we have any control? Check (✔) them off and cross out the rest.	How do we think that these variables are interrelated with one another? With what effect?	What should we do about them?
1.			Please don't rush to fill in this part of the conversation. This is typical "fix it" trap of the older mechanical thinking. Keep reading the book and learning to understand your situation and enjoy the conversation with your leaders along the way.
2.			
3.			
4.			

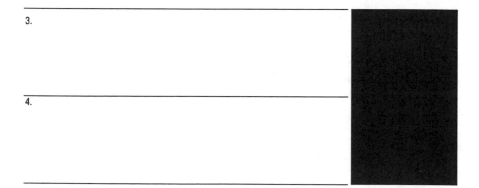

B.   A congregation is an organism that naturally seeks balance and equilibrium.

What "resistance" have we experienced in recent attempts of change?	What *information* or *learnings* can be found in this attempt to re-balance your system?	What should you do about it?
1.		See the caution about rushing to "do" in the example above.
2.		
3.		
4.		

C. A congregation is an organism in which the parts and the whole interact.

As leaders, what have we been learning about our congregation that would be helpful for others to learn?	As leaders what have we been feeling or experiencing that would be helpful for us and others to talk about?	Who specifically (which "others"?) needs to do the learning?

1.

2.

3.

4.

CHAPTER 4

Welcome to the Wilderness: The Spiritual Journey of Congregational Change

"But even more important," he said, "is the way complex systems seem to strike a balance between the need for order and the imperative to change. Complex systems tend to locate themselves at a place we call 'the edge of chaos.' We imagine the edge of chaos as a place where there is enough innovation to keep a living system vibrant, and enough stability to keep it from collapsing into anarchy. It is a zone of conflict and upheaval, where the old and the new are constantly at war. Finding the balance must be a delicate matter.... Only at the edge of chaos can complex systems flourish."
                                        –Michael Crichton, *The Lost World*

The pastor had been at the congregation for less than two years and was generally thought of very highly. As a matter of fact, in her last evaluation she was rated highly in all areas except two. And in those areas, she still received scores in the 90 percent range on the instrument they were using for evaluation. Yet she was constantly under criticism by some members of the governing board, and board meetings were largely unproductive and negative. The president of the board did not know what to do so decided to have a "hearing of concerns" and during one meeting invited the board members to list all their concerns and complaints on newsprint. The response was demoralizing. The board listed thirty concerns—all complaints, most aimed at their pastor, who was identified as the cause or as having failed to provide the solution.

The pastor and the president wrestled with their response for the next meeting. Should they defend themselves or the pastor in light of the complaints? Should the pastor simply resign, despite the obvious support and appreciation the congregation seemed to hold for her? How could all these problems, many of them longstanding, be addressed to the satisfaction of the more vocal board members?

Instead of trying to defend against or correct the perceptions of the board members, the pastor and president decided they would help the board feel its own pain and not try to take them off the hook by assuming all responsibility for the "list of thirty." They went into the next board meeting with a written report for the board to discuss.

The first section of the report was "Historical Issues." This included all items on the list of thirty complaints that appeared in the minutes or actions of any of six key leadership groups in the church over the past ten years. In columns next to each complaint were check marks to indicate which groups had discussed or taken action on each issue. It was easy to see by the check marks that all of the items in this section had been discussed or given attention by a number of groups in the congregation over the years. Eighteen of the thirty items on the original list of concerns were included, indicating the issues had a history that far preceded the arrival of their new pastor. The pastor and president invited the board members to discuss the question, Why have we not been successful or effective in addressing these concerns in the past?

The second section of the form was "New Issues" and included the remainder of the concerns, which seemed to have arisen since the new pastor arrived. Next to each of the concerns on this section of the report were columns where check marks could be placed to identify who (one or more people or groups) had primary responsibility to address the item. The pastor and president invited a conversation for this section of the report: Who has responsibility to provide leadership around each of these concerns? The outcome of this conversation was agreement that less than a handful of issues directly related to the pastor's role or performance, and that most of the concerns were shared leadership issues that belonged to one or more leadership groups. The pastor and board members agreed that the pastor would develop specific plans addressing the items that were directly her responsibility, and board members would do the same with the concerns listed as their responsibility.

It was not a quick and easy solution. In fact, the board members were now more uncomfortable than before, because they could not

*make their pastor the scapegoat for their concerns and they now had
a much clearer picture of the real situation. But increasingly, board
members became interested in talking about what they could do or
what they could learn to help the situation, rather than just complaining. The change process was beginning.*

In this chapter I want to talk about why it took Moses forty years to
cross the wilderness when he could have made it in less than forty months
had he taken a straighter path. And I want to take a look at why some
congregations will take a long time to work their way through their own
wilderness of changes facing them, rather than move quickly to the next
solution. The contrast has to do with the depth of the change and the difference between linear and chaotic change.

The difference is anything but simple or subtle. It is not just "semantics." For example, there really is a difference between the words
leadership and *management,* as outlined in an earlier chapter, and these
words and ideas are not interchangeable. As I noted, a time of deep
change calls for leadership more than management. And there really is
a difference between long-range planning and strategic planning. Long-
range planning assumes that what your congregation is doing is faithful
to your call and meets the needs of your members and community.
Long-range planners ask, What's next? and assume that what went before has been appropriate. Strategic planners asks very different questions, such as Who are we? and, What have we been called to do in our
ministry? The questions are different because strategic planners do not
assume that all that has happened in the history of the congregation is
appropriate to the present day. So strategic planners dig deeper, examin-
ing more fundamental and foundational understandings of the congregation. And, therefore, it is more difficult to do.

Management and leadership. Long-range planning and strategic
planning. Linear and chaotic change. It is not just semantics. It has much
to do with the depth or magnitude of change a congregation is facing. In
times of moderate change, when basic stability is assumed, management,
long-range planning, and linear models of change are effective and appropriate. But when change occurs at a deeper level, when stability and
continuity cannot be assumed, deeper responses are required. And so we
turn to leadership, strategic planning, and chaotic models or understandings of change.

What lens of change do we use to look at our congregations to understand what we are dealing with and what might be the appropriate response of leaders? Do we look at the congregation through a *linear* lens or a *chaotic* lens? The way we look at our congregation in the midst of change will determine the response we offer as leaders.

A Linear Lens

Perhaps the model of change with which we are all most familiar is linear problem solving. It follows a basic pattern:

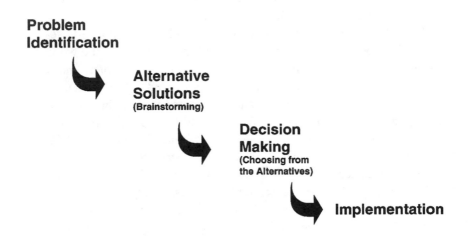

**Problem
Identification**

**Alternative
Solutions**
(Brainstorming)

**Decision
Making**
(Choosing from
the Alternatives)

Implementation

This is the basic problem-solving methodology that has been taught to us from "day one,"and we can assume that if you have been chosen or ordained to be a leader of your congregation, you know this model and use it often. And for good reason: It works.

Problem Identification

We know that if we can get people to agree on what the problem actually is, then we are well on the way to solving it and working our way through the change required. Carefully defining the problem so everyone understands and is satisfied with the definition is a key step in helping people to accept and support the change that they are facing.

Alternative Solutions

Brainstorming, or developing a list of alternative solutions or approaches to the change facing a congregation, is a necessary and effective step in responding to an identified problem. It invites people to be creative and to look at alternative approaches that might not be obvious at the outset. It invites people to express concern as well as enthusiasm about what might need to change in order to address the problems. And, most importantly, it invites people to own the solution because they have participated in developing their own response to the situation.

Decision Making and Implementation

If the problem is well identified and alternative solutions are developed, the task of decision making (choosing the most appropriate or effective solution) and implementation of the solution tend to follow directly.

For example, in 1977 a rather large church building burned down in what was described as a case of either arson or a child's fire-play that got out of hand. The congregation had fewer than fifty active members, many of the members were in their seventies, and many years before most of the members had moved out of the community where the church building was located and returned only on Sundays to attend worship. Once the shock and the grief had worn off a bit, it was very clear to all concerned that this congregation was not going to rebuild on the site of their burned facility and try to continue ministry in that place. Members were too old and there were too few members to begin again. It was agreed that the "problem" they faced was what to do as a congregation (a faith community) without a church (a building).

After just a few meetings they agreed they had essentially three alternatives. They could search for a smaller, less costly, and more conveniently located facility in which to continue as a congregation, and this option might include sharing space with another congregation. Or they could merge with another local congregation of the same denomination. Or they could disband.

When exploring the alternatives, they discovered that their central concerns were that they remain together as a group to preserve their relationships, and that they not take on more than they could handle at their age and level of interest. They, therefore, quickly dismissed the option of disbanding and the option of relocating in some other space because those options did not address their concerns. They accepted the alternative of merger as one that allowed them to stay together as a group but did not require them to take on all of the responsibilities and labors of "running" a congregation by themselves. Their decision, which was reached with full accord, was to send out messages to the surrounding congregations of their denomination indicating they would welcome invitations for merger from any who were interested in the possibility. And they set about working with the congregations that responded to find the place that suited all parties best. The cause of the changes they faced was traumatic. The amount of change they faced was extensive. But the experience was managed by clarifying the real issues and options and making the necessary choices.

The linear model of change works. But it works best under certain conditions:

- when the problem is clear and not complex, and
- when there is a low level of conflict regarding the situation.

This is a "technical" situation (as was discussed in chapter 2). When there is a clear problem and leaders can surface one or more clear solutions, then it is appropriate to move and to implement the change. People may need some help to understand and accept the change, but the linear problem-solving model works.

A Chaos Lens

But what about deeper levels of change? We are increasingly experiencing examples of change much too complex and unclear to be served well by the linear problem-solving model. Many leaders in congregations today are trying to address deeper, more confusing change that does not present clear problems or solutions. In such a situation, the use of a linear model is not effective and it can be destructive. Consider a historic congregation that boasts of being one of the oldest Protestant congregations in the United States. Members include long-term residents of the community, some of whom can trace their ancestry back to early colonial settlers. As a group, the long-term members of this congregation tend to share the community disdain for the "newcomers" who have moved into the area over recent years. They are not at all pleased by the new housing projects that now dot their landscape. The congregation has been experiencing declines in membership and average worship attendance for the past thirty years. Visitors seem to come and go in this congregation, but few become active members. And there has been substantial infighting between long-term leaders and newer leaders.

Although this scenario is not unusual by any means, it is somewhat complex and invites disagreement and conflict as people seek to understand what is "wrong." The response of congregational leaders to date, however, has been to apply the simpler linear model of change. They have simply said that the "problem" is their clergy, who have proven to be ineffective in turning their situation around. It is not surprising the congregation now has its fourth new pastor in only six years: The congregation is not dealing with the depth of the change it is facing.

To more effectively address their situation, these leaders would do well to look at it through a *chaotic* model of change to understand what is required of them. A chaotic model begins with an understanding of change that recognizes the reality and the value of a time of chaos (messiness, lack of clarity, a need for wandering). In a most helpful article John Scherer, president of John Scherer Associates and former president of the Association of Creative Change, has written:

> No significant change can take place in individuals, groups, or larger organizations, regardless of the pain and possibility present, without a passage through chaos, the world's "birthing center," where fundamental change and innovation come into being.[1]

Scherer's model of change acknowledges chaos and offers a new way to understand what congregations need to go through in order to deal creatively and faithfully with deeper levels of change, such as those they face in times of large paradigmatic swings. The steps or stages in this model are as follows:

Pain
  ↳ (plus)
      ↳**Possibility**
          ↳ (minus)
              ↳ **The Box**
                  ↳ (will lead to)
                      ↳ **Chaos—The Wilderness**
                          ↳ (where we will be helped to find)
                              ↳ **The Creative and**
                                 Faithful Choice

As we did with the linear model of change, let's consider the various stages of this way of looking at change.

Pain

Scherer defines "pain" as the "awareness of an unacceptable disequilibrium, or a significant discrepancy between the way things ARE and the way things COULD BE."[2] The pain does not necessarily need to "hurt." But it is an awareness of a pinch point that something is amiss or there is a gap between the current situation and what might be expected or what you are used to experiencing. It might be a sudden awareness that the pews on Sunday are no longer as full as they once were. Curiously, for many congregations the decline in attendance may have been going on for quite a few years, but people suddenly become aware that members are gone and there are no new members to replace them. Somehow this realization catches up to people in an awakening moment and they are suddenly "aware." This is pain.

It may be the realization at the end of a stewardship or a membership drive that the congregation will be facing the third deficit budget in the same number of years. It may be the realization that the nominations committee had to invite more than fifty members in order to find two members willing to be nominated to the governing board (a very painful example from one congregation). It may be the "warfare" that is going on between the clergy, the music director, and the congregation about which hymns get sung from the recently purchased new edition of the denominational hymnal. It may be the disagreement between newer and older members about which programs will get the support of congregational mission dollars. Whatever the discomforts, the pain alerts the leaders and the congregation that something is not "right."

In a time of more modest change, and using a linear model, the pain might simply be perceived as a "problem" and leaders might begin to look about for a solution. When faced with deeper change in the life of the congregation, however, the pain is not to be "solved." It is to be preserved and clarified, for *pain provides motivation*. The feeling that something is not right, that there is something amiss that cannot be easily changed, motivates people. It gives them a reason and a purpose for hanging in there to work at deeper levels to see what is going on. The case study at the beginning of this chapter, in which the governing board was able to brainstorm thirty concerns they wanted to lay at the feet of their senior pastor, is an example of using "pain" for motivation instead of seeking a solution. Had the board been allowed to approach this as a problem to be solved, they would have concluded that they had the wrong senior pastor and gone in search of a new one, without changing any of the root causes of long-term issues. Or, perhaps equally damaging, the senior pastor might have assumed they were right about her ineptness and set about changing herself to solve their problems and ending up less authentic than she really is.

Instead, the senior pastor and the president of the board listened carefully and did their homework. They identified which concerns actually belonged to the senior pastor, so she could learn how to address them and become more effective as this congregation's pastoral leader. But they also identified which issues belonged to the governing board and to the history of the congregation and gave them back to the board to wrestle with. Were the board members pleased with this response? Not particularly. They would have preferred that someone had solved their perceived problems. And, in fact, there were a few holdouts who insisted that it really was the senior pastor's "fault" and that she was just passing the buck. But a significant number of board members were a bit surprised, and they sat up and took notice. In other words, they were suddenly *motivated* to look deeper and to try to figure out what was really going on and what part they had to play in it. It has been about one and a half years now since those initial meetings over "problems," and everything is far from settled. But the relationship between the senior pastor and the governing board has changed significantly, and together they have changed the way they are looking at the possibilities for the future of their church. Not easy work, but it would have been impossible to make progress if they had used a linear model of change and looked for easy solutions.

Helping a congregation or a group of leaders become aware of their "pain" is a delicate and a creative task. It is much more than simply announcing "bad news." The clergyperson or the membership chairperson who goes to the meeting of the governing board with charts of the membership for the last ten years to "prove" that they have been losing members and concludes by announcing, "We'd better do something to turn this around or else we'll be out of business in another ten years," is more likely to be met with defensiveness and anger than with motivation to do something. On the other hand, taking the same charts to the meeting, not with admonishments but with questions for the board to discuss, such as "How aware have we been of this trend over past years?" and "What are the implications of this trend for our future ministry?" can be much more engaging and motivating, although still discomforting.

As mentioned before, we all have our own biases and assumptions out of which we tell our histories. Congregations are no different. We remember and tell our stories most often in a favorable light and, at times, need to be helped by leaders to see the reality that can be hidden by our assumptions. In other words, it is common for congregations to want to explain away their pain as unrelated to their own doings and therefore something beyond their control. Although they may be right to an extent (remember, 50 to 60 percent of the variables that impact a congregation are beyond its control), leadership still needs to help the congregation to own its pain in order to be motivated to address the reality of the situation.

This denial of circumstances was obvious in the planning work one mid-sized, center-city congregation in a small Eastern city was doing. I had asked them to prepare the standard graphs of their membership and average attendance for the past twenty years. At a subsequent meeting of the governing board, we were all looking at charts with descending lines indicating a long decline in the size of this congregation. But for some reason the conversation did not feel as if it was ringing true for me as I listened to them minimize the impact of this obvious history. There were about twenty-five people present, and I asked them to break up into five small groups and to complete the graph by drawing the lines five years into the future "with the assumption that you make no major changes in the programs or priorities of your congregation." Remarkably four of the five small groups returned after fifteen minutes with graphs showing marked upswings in the lines they projected for the next five years. When invited to talk about why they concluded it was appropriate to predict membership growth for the next five years when looking at membership decline for the past twenty years, each of the small groups came up with a version of "we don't know, but something will happen." These leaders needed help to face reality. They needed help and support in feeling their pain so they would not be overwhelmed by it and feel helpless. They also needed help to try not to solve their problem quickly and make it go away, so that they would be able to learn from it.

Possibility

Pain is the awareness of an unacceptable disequilibrium, and possibility is recognizing something that could be achieved. Possibility is a description of a healthier state of being. As Scherer describes it, "The overweight person must actually see himself leaner and more healthy. The work team or organization must see the possibility of the situation resolved, productivity at peak levels, the crisis yielding to breakthrough."[3] For the congregation, possibility may mean seeing the possibility of the bickering at board meetings giving way to a sense of community, or the congregation accepting people with obvious differences not only into membership but also into leadership, or the ministry of a congregation no longer being constrained by lack of money, not because money magically becomes more available but because the way they approach their ministry becomes more creative and collaborative. Possibilities, like visioning within a congregation, draw the picture of what could be—without yet knowing how to get there. And heathy possibilities are those that match the beliefs and the values of the congregation.

Pain provides motivation, and possibilities *provide motivation and direction*. In order to cope with significant change, a system needs to at least know in what direction it is hoping to go. Was it Yogi Berra who said, "If you don't know where you're going, you'll probably end up someplace else"? We need some sense of direction in order to know how and where to begin our work. Possibilities do not tell us how to get there, but they begin to shape or draw the picture of the destination, so we at least know in which general direction we are called to explore.

Pain and Possibility

We need to look more closely at the relationship between pain and possibility. Scherer calls these the "parents" of change. Both must be present, offering both motivation and direction, in order for deeper change to be attempted by the leaders of a congregation. As leaders work with their congregations, they must assess what is needed. Do leaders need to help members have a clearer sense of the pain they are facing, so members will be willing to walk into an unclear future? Or do members need a clearer sense of the real possibility or possibilities that might lie ahead, so that they will know something about where they are seeking to go? Leaders need to make judgments to respond to what is needed to move the congregation forward.

But leaders need to be very careful that the possibilities they surface and explore do not look like "answers." Pain met with something that looks like an "answer" will feel very much like a problem that has a solution. And a governing board that is feeling pain will quickly move to a solution to restabilize itself (to restore the system's equilibrium), even if the solution will not work. Latching on to a false solution or answer will rob the congregation of the motivation and direction provided by pain and possibility by allowing people to think that they have solved their problem.

In one congregation the governing board was experiencing growing concern and frustration about the lack of money. As this issue was being discussed at one meeting, a board member made the statement, "What we need are more members." He spoke of the declining membership of the congregation over the past years, the shrinking attendance at worship, and the need for more "giving units" to support the budget. This conversation quickly snowballed into a recommendation that a part-time minister of evangelism be hired using available interest from an endowment fund. The board members talked about the need to "bring in new members" from the neighborhood and assured themselves that the increased giving from additional members would offset any costs for the new staff person by the second, or at least the third, year. Although there was no formal action taken that evening to hire additional staff, there was a feeling of consensus that this was the appropriate direction to go, and board members left the meeting thinking they had "solved their problem."

The congregation, however, was like so many others: Many of the active members had moved away from the congregation's neighborhood twenty to forty years earlier. A good portion of the active members were loyal people who continued to drive ten to forty minutes back into this neighborhood for worship, social events, and meetings. They had lost their contact with the neighborhood years before and had received almost no new members from the immediately surrounding area for the past ten years. By proposing to hire a staff person in evangelism to bring in new members from the neighborhood, they had hit upon a "solution" that had little prospect of success. They would be asking a part-time person, who would probably not live in that neighborhood, to build relationships with people they had lived beside but ignored for decades. And because the task of evangelism would be given to the new staff person, the leaders and members of the congregation (including the senior pastor) would be off the hook for meeting, greeting, and inviting people they did not know and whom they suspected were different from them. The pain of their declining budget support and membership would be relieved by the application of a solution that was guaranteed not to change them.

The course of the meeting, and the future of this congregation, would have been quite different if leaders in this situation had first helped the board to become sensitive to its pain, perhaps by doing a bit of homework on their current membership. Building a pin map by placing a pin on a large map to mark the address of every household that belonged to the church might have helped leaders to see clearly whom their ministry was currently attracting and serving. By using a different colored pin for the last fifty to seventy-five new members, they might have been inspired to talk about where their new members were coming from and begun to guess what brought these new people to their congregation.

It is very instructive for leaders to know who has been joining the congregation over the most recent months or years and then to ask, "Why?" As leaders became more familiar with which parts of the larger community are served by their congregation, and what their latest new members look like and what they were seeking when they came to this congregation, the conversation about possibilities might be quite different from and healthier than the usual conversations.

For example, they might have begun to explore the possibility of "building a bridge across our driveway" as one Roman Catholic congregation did when they explored inviting people from the immediate neighborhood into their church. Their homework around their pain had convinced them that there was an invisible barrier that kept neighborhood people from walking across the driveway into their building, so they began to explore the possibility of membership that had a "bridge" over the driveway that would allow these nearest of neighbors in. Over a period of time this possibility of a bridge to new membership took on interesting characteristics in this church. Since a good portion of the surrounding neighborhood was African American, this Roman Catholic parish began intentionally to elect more African Americans to their parish council so that neighbors could see that they were welcome there. And during a renovation of the sanctuary a number of angels on the ceiling and several mural figures on the walls were repainted having black skin so that these new neighbors would know that this was a place where they, too, could worship God. The pain that was met with possibility in this congregation provided no easy solution or comfort. But the gradual learning about what it takes to live out the possibility of a membership that bridges into the neighborhood provided energy and direction that the other church had quickly short-circuited by a recommendation to be staff-dependent on a minister of evangelism who would have been given an impossible task, however much relief it might have offered to the immediate pain of a budget problem.

Without pain there is no motivation. Without possibility there is no direction in which people can address their pain. The point, however, is that when faced with deeper changes, the possibilities that follow a congregation's awareness of its pain cannot look or sound too much like a solution, or all motivation and direction will be lost. Both pain and possibility must be present if change is to be born. And pain and possibility cannot be presented as if they are problems to be solved.

Minus the Box

When leaders are able to introduce their board or congregation appropriately to its pain, and when they are able to draw pictures of alternative
possibilities that suggest where leaders might search and learn, the next
step in a chaotic model of change is to help people escape from their
boxes. Take a moment to play the games below. (The answers to these
games can be found in the endnotes for this chapter.[4])

A Game

You may play these games alone. If you play them with other
leaders, however, invite everyone to find their own solutions
first, and then compare results.

1. Connect all nine dots in the following drawing by using four
straight lines and without taking your pencil off the paper. (This
is an old standard.)

2. In the following line of letters, cross out six letters so that the
remaining letters, without altering their sequence, will spell a familiar English word.

BSAINXLEATNTEARS

Now that you have had a chance to play with the two games and have found answers (did you have to look in the endnote to get the answers?), do you see that the answers depended upon breaking out of mental boxes that hide solutions? In the game with the nine dots, the outer dots form a box in our minds. It is a principle of Gestalt psychology that when our minds are presented with an incomplete picture, we fill in the rest. So nine dots, in fact, look like a box to us. To solve the problem by staying inside the "box" with four straight lines is impossible. You have to break out of the box for a solution. (By the way, if you break out of a few more boxes, there are also ways to connect the nine dots using three straight lines without taking your pencil off the paper; two straight lines without taking your pencil off the paper; and one straight line without taking your pencil off the paper. Why not play a little longer and try it?) Similarly, the instruction to crossing out the six letters invites us to break out of the boxes of language. The more natural tendency is to play inside the mental box by finding the "right" letters to cross out instead of literally following directions and crossing out the letters S-I-X-L-E-T-T-E-R and S.

In the same way, if congregations are going to address deeper levels of change, we need to help ourselves, other leaders, and members to break out of our boxes about congregations. The boxes are assumptions about the situation we are facing. Or they are assumptions about the way congregations work and have always worked. Or they are assumptions about the way we are going to find our solutions or next steps to deal with the issues facing us. Once again, our mind and our experience draw boxes, using the incomplete data that face us, and we are locked into thinking as we have always thought and behaving as we have always behaved. The old adage comes back to haunt us: "When we don't know what else to do, we do what we know." Yet we cannot address deep change or solve complex riddles by staying inside the old boxes.

To help ourselves and our leaders to break out of our boxes takes some creativity and some risk. When you suggest that they risk a new approach, people are going to wonder why you are doing something so different ("Ms. Chairperson, why are you wasting our time with these games?") But what if you:

•   asked the board to meet in the lounge or in someone's living room? (Board members that meet in board rooms tend to act as if they are at board meetings.)

• led a discussion about issues facing your church with a prestated "rule" that no decisions will be entertained or allowed as part of the discussion? (Board members who cannot make decisions do not feel like they are really at a board meeting.)

• asked everyone not to make a second point or speak a second time until everyone has shared a comment or opinion? (Board members tend to defer to the most outspoken members of the group, and it does not occur to them that everyone has an opinion.)

• arranged for groups of leaders to visit congregations very dissimilar to yours, provided time for them to talk with leaders of those congregations about why their practice, strategy, or mission is important and effective for them, and then provided time back home for the leaders to talk with one another about their learnings?

• arranged for a group of leaders to visit with you in your home, made them some popcorn, and showed them:

   — the movie *Sister Act* and at the end invited them to talk about the purpose of worship; or
   — a rerun of *Northern Exposure* and at the end invited them to talk about the meaning and characteristics of community; or
   — (what else can you think of that gets at the issue facing them but is outside their box?)

• led a Bible study in which you did not try to learn new facts about the Bible but used the Bible to teach you something new about yourself? For example, ask your board what biblical story they think your congregation is living out right now, and then read the details of that story carefully to look for information about yourself. (See the case study at the beginning of chapter 2.)

• did not stop with these examples but you thought of your own creative way to help yourself and your leaders to step outside of the boxes to take a fresh look at your congregation's situation?

Helping yourself and other congregational leaders to step outside of the assumptions and experiences that have always guided your congregation is essential to addressing deeper change. As Scherer writes:

> There are conscious and unconscious forces at work in all human systems, from the individual to the largest corporation, which function to maintain homeostasis, keeping things as they are. When we think and perceive the world within a closed system, we are doing "inside the box thinking." Standing inside the box, there is no real possibility for fundamental change. There might be change, but inside-the-box change is more of the same, only different.[5]

Chaos (the Wilderness)

Having become sensitive to what is incomplete or missing (the pain), having risked drawing new possibilities for the way things might faithfully be, having worked past our assumptions about how things must be in order to step out of our box, our hope is to be able to find our "solution" and move on from all this hard work. But instead we are delivered into the chaos.

> For transformation to occur, the existing mental box must fall away like the discarded skin on a molting snake. The operating pattern must be broken down. We must find ourselves released from the grip of the old context. This leaves us, not immediately with a new pattern, but with *empty space* within which a new pattern (creation) can occur. In other words, we must find ourselves in a *chaotic void,* without any life jacket or props or ideas about how to proceed, with nothing to hold on to, no way to save ourselves. In that instant, we are open to what *could* show up, which could *not* have shown up as long as we were holding on to anything we thought would "save us from the experience of being in an empty space.[6]

When we talk about change in continuing education events at the Alban Institute, it is at this point that I invite the participants to do two things. The first is to hold on. Before we let our anxieties and emotional reactivity kick in and subvert the work of change, we need to hear the rest of the story and consider that ending up in chaos can be the product of effective and faithful leadership. The second thing I invite leaders to do is not go back home to their congregation and announce that it is time to walk into chaos.

The fact is that few, if any, of us are anxious to walk into chaos, where answers are hidden and rules are unknown. Chaos is not welcome in our personal lives, marriages, or friendships, and certainly not in our congregations. In fact, one of the issues leaders need to attend to in times of deep change is the management of the fear (their own and the congregation's) of having little control and few answers.

But chaos is creative space. We should not miss the implications for us that in Genesis, the world is understood to be created out of chaos. When a system is held in chaos long enough, the system approaches the threshold of substantive change that could not be reached in any other fashion. This is one of the central learnings of the new physics, which works at the subatomic level. It was discovered that a molecule held in chaos can be brought to a condition of excitement and self-regulation that will allow it to reorganize at a higher level. Through the work of physicist and Nobel laureate Ilya Prigogene, the phenomena of *self-renewal* and *self-transcendence* were discovered as principles of self-organizing systems.[7] A system that is in chaos long enough will self-organize. It will renew itself and transcend beyond its former self to accommodate and relate much more effectively with its new environment. The principles suggest that when there are no clear answers or easy solutions to the dilemmas that face many of our congregations, the responsible act of leadership is to help hold the congregation in the chaos of not knowing what to do next, so that new possibilities of creation, which would have been hidden, might surface.

This is not an easy act of leadership. It means facing one's fears and becoming comfortable with (even enjoying?) the failures that are an inevitable by-product of searching in the midst of chaos. And it means unhooking oneself from one's own fears and failures. The fact is that as leaders, we are not the cause of the chaos many of our congregations are facing. We need to unhook ourselves from the responsibility of always understanding what is going on, and from the fear of not having the answer to solve the problem quickly.

Yet unhooking from the fear of and the need to be responsible for the chaos a congregation faces is liberating and itself allows for the

promise of new creation that was not there before. I was working with a
friend who had recently become the chaplain of a well-known university
campus ministry and who was following two predecessors who had gone
on from that post to high profile and powerful positions. The campus
ministry itself was facing major challenges, and my friend was overwhelmed by what he believed he could not do—that is, keep up with the
reputation of his predecessors and prepare to move this ministry to a
more successful level. We talked for several months, during which time
I thought my friend was becoming increasingly depressed. And then in
our next conversation my friend was himself again, with energy, enthusiasm, and a host of new ideas to work on as leader of this ministry. I
asked what had happened to him that made such a change. "I went back
and read the minutes of the board meetings for the past seven years," he
said. "And I read month after month how they tried something and it
failed, or how someone had a great idea that everyone supported, but
they couldn't get any volunteers to actually attempt it, or they planned
a great program to address a clear need that the students said they felt
but no one came. After I read that for seven years," he told me, " I said
to myself, 'Hell, I can do that!'" Having been set free from fear, and
having recognized the chaos the ministry had been in for years, both my
friend and the board were set free to reorganize at a higher level. The
effectiveness of their efforts to reorganize could be measured several
years later at least in part by the significant number of people who en-
tered ordained ministry as an outgrowth of their participation in that
campus ministry. Had the chaplain not faced his fears and let go to live
in the chaos of his situation, the reorganization of the ministry probably
would not have happened.

The Creative and Faithful Choice

There seems to be fairly broad agreement that congregations are living
in "the time between paradigms," as described by Loren Mead. This
suggests that we do not know clearly what the creative and faithful
choices will be for a lot of congregations. As Mead says, "Neither the
new age nor the new paradigm has arrived, so we are pulled by the new
and constrained by the old without the privilege even of knowing fully
what the new will be like."[8]

But what is clear is that congregations and middle judicatory systems that have been faithfully living in the chaos of contemporary ministry are self-organizing in new and creative ways that are not the simple outgrowth of older assumptions and patterns of congregational life. A United Methodist congregation in Pennsylvania has informal Saturday evening worship services, because it came to understand that it was now living in the middle of a large concentration of young adults who grew up in the Roman Catholic Church, but who were now inactive and would not be likely to walk into a United Methodist worship service on Sunday mornings. The Saturday evening service provided a time that was familiar and allowed for an informality that was attractive to these young adults. An Episcopal church in California has a Sunday evening vesper service that begins with half an hour of yoga because the congregation is doing ministry in a community that understands yoga but does not understand vespers. A small urban congregation with a very old membership is supporting its pastor in leading worship and educational events with a focus on creation spirituality, which they clearly state they do not understand or personally respond to but which they see as a way of continuing their ministry with a new generation of members who now come to the church because they do understand and resonate with creation spirituality. A suburban congregation has very few elected leaders because of the lack of volunteer time available to its members. So just a few people make the decisions but offer regular bimonthly, all-member "town meetings" in which leaders commit themselves to listening to the joys and concerns of the members.

In each of these cases, and so many more, the congregations have had to break out of their boxes about how congregations live and work. They have taken their pain and their possibilities seriously and have sought to be faithful in new ways. The way is not clear. There is still a tremendous amount of discomfort in these congregations as they wonder whether they have gone too far and "capitulated to the marketplace" of people's interests, and in the process diminished the practice of their faith. Denominational officials also feel some discomfort because they have encouraged and supported local congregations to stretch and revision their ministry in creative ways, only to wonder whether a congregation is now so different that it no longer fits within the denominational family.

But the change in these and a host of other congregations is a deep expression of their faithfulness. And it is change they would not have found if they had simply tried to solve their problems instead of learning from their pain, dreaming new possibilities, breaking out of boxes, and learning to live in the wilderness of chaos.

Where Does Moses Fit into All This?

I began this chapter saying that I wanted to address why it took Moses forty years to cross the wilderness instead of forty months or less, which would have been possible if a more direct path had been chosen. When considering deep change that faces our congregations, Moses seems to be a rather apt model of both leadership and change. Some of the learnings that have helped us to understand chaos have come from the new sciences. We can also learn from older lessons that come from the stories of our faith. Our faith stories tell us that God is to be encountered in the wilderness, where we do not exercise control and do not know all the rules. From the Israelites wandering in the desert for forty years, to Jesus spending forty days and forty nights in the wilderness, the creative and teaching nature of chaos is deep in our faith experience.

In part, these stories teach us that as our congregations face great change, it is God who does the transforming, not one or two leaders who somehow know what the answer is. In the Exodus story it is written, "Then the Lord God said, *I* have observed the misery…, *I* have heard their cry…, *I* have come down to deliver them from the Egyptians…." (Exodus 3:7-8). The migration from Egypt to a promised land was not the vision brought to the people from the wise and wonderful leader, Moses, who knew better and saw farther. The migration happened as an act of transformation by the hand of God.

And it took forty years in chaos, the wilderness, because the people needed the time to reorganize at a higher level. Had they made the trip in forty weeks or forty months, the people of Israel would have arrived in the promised land unchanged. They would still have been a slave people, still behaving like a slave people. But during forty years of being held in the wilderness, they were transformed into a people that had a new relationship with God in which they had learned dependence on God, even for their daily food. They had a new identity and understanding of self and a new way of organizing their community with a set of

commandments and a structure for decision making that went beyond
Moses and Aaron. Those who went into the wilderness as a group of
slaves came out as a nation looking for a promised home in which they
could live independently.

The Bible leads us to the same conclusions as do the new sciences.
To be a leader in a situation of deep change is to hold the people in the
chaos or the wilderness long enough for transformation to take place.
To be a leader in a situation of deep change does not require the ability
to produce an answer. It requires the patience and the courage to hold
people without an answer close to the pain and possibility that can transform. In an enchanting and provoking midrash, Rabbi Lawrence Kushner
wonders why a God who can split the sea, create pillars of fire, and
make the sun stand still resorts to a cheap parlor trick like a burning
bush to call Moses as a leader for his people.[9] The answer is that the
burning bush that was not consumed was not a miracle, it was a test.
God was testing Moses' attention span. It takes several minutes for a
person to watch the bush burning to discover that it is not being consumed. Those who glanced at the bush and looked away would see only
a burning bush. Kushner says, "God wanted to find out whether or not
Moses could pay attention to something for more than a few minutes.
When Moses did, God spoke. The trick is to pay attention to what is going on around you long enough to behold the miracle without falling
asleep." The trick of leadership in a chaotic time is to pay attention and
hold still long enough for significant change to occur.

The role of the leader is to pay attention long enough and not run
off to fix something. It is to help people confront their pain, disappointments, and anxieties without diminishing them but also without being
overwhelmed by them. It is to help people dream dreams of alternate
possibilities that provide direction and energy. It is to help people escape the boxes of their assumptions and learned behavior so that deep
change is not subverted by old rules. And, perhaps most importantly, it
is to help hold people in the wilderness of their experience, the chaos of
not knowing what comes next until it comes. It is what Ronald Heifetz
in his remarkable book on leadership describes as providing a "holding
environment" for containing the stresses of adaptive change.[10] The
stresses are real. It is important to remember that "on the fifteenth day
of the second month after they had departed from the land of Egypt, the
whole congregation of the Israelites complained against Moses and

Aaron in the wilderness," saying, "If only we had died by the hand of the Lord in the land of Egypt...; for you have brought us out into this wilderness to kill this whole assembly with hunger" (Exodus 16:1-2). In other words, forty-five days into a forty-year journey, the people were asking, "Are we there yet?" It may have been a reasonable question, because forty-five days was plenty of time to get there. But it was not a complaint that needed a quick response from leaders to make people happy. The example Moses offers is of a leader who trusts God sufficiently to hold the people in the wilderness long enough for God to provide deep change.

The Leadership Response

In order to provide leadership, people need to ask themselves what kind of a situation their congregation is facing. Is the problem clear? Can possible solutions be found in our common experience? Do we face a situation of relatively low conflict and relatively high shared understanding? If so, the steps and stages of linear problem solving are appropriate. The role of leaders is then to take action. Clarify the problem so that people agree on what is to be changed. Brainstorm alternative solutions and decide which is most appropriate. Then bring together the resources needed to implement the solution.

But if the situation facing the congregation is more complex and less clear, a very different response is needed from leaders, one that acknowledges the chaos that is necessarily a part of the change. A key task of leaders is to have some clear sense of what kind of a situation they are facing and then providing what is needed by the congregation. Knowing what is needed and offering an appropriate response is enabled by looking at the congregation through the right lens.

Exercises for Leaders

The following diagnostic conversations are meant to invite an intuitive awareness of where your congregation may be in the process of change and what is needed from leaders. Invite a group of leaders to use their own experience and information to test whether there is agreement on what the congregation is facing.

When answering the question, Where do you think your congregation is? think about the critical mass of the people in the congregation. It is common to find individuals in the congregation who can be identified with each point or stage in descriptive models such as these. It is not particularly helpful to identify where individuals may be unless there is a need to help certain individuals move past a stage where they may have become active blockers of change. Describing where most of the people in the congregation are usually helps leaders know what the congregation needs.

1. Identify one or more critical issues facing your congregation. Try to determine whether the congregation is facing *linear change* or *chaotic change*.

Linear change

- The problem is clear and not complex.
- There is a low level of conflict regarding the situation.

Chaotic change

- The problem is less clear with few, if any, clear solutions.
- The problem is sufficiently complex and there is enough dis agreement that people do not know quite how to determine a "solution."

Invite participants to begin by writing personal notes about ex amples or evidence that show why the situation facing your congregation fits better with one model of change than the other. Lead a discussion among participants, inviting them to use their notes to describe the change that faces the congregation.

2. Using the outlines of the two models of change below:

A. Go to the model of change that you have agreed best fits your congregation based on your conversation in step 1 above.

B. Discuss where you think your congregation is within that model. Which step or stage of the change model do you think the critical mass of your congregation is experiencing at the moment? (Use examples to explain why.)

C. Discuss what you think would be appropriate and helpful responses from leaders, using the description in this chapter of that step or stage.

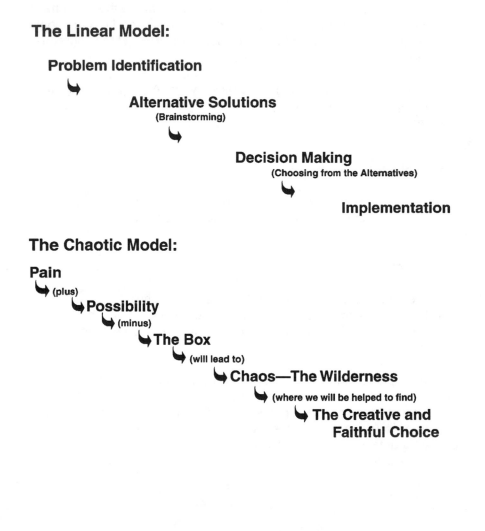

The Linear Model:

Problem Identification
↳
    Alternative Solutions
    (Brainstorming)
    ↳
        Decision Making
        (Choosing from the Alternatives)
        ↳
           Implementation

The Chaotic Model:

Pain
↳ (plus)
  ↳**Possibility**
  ↳ (minus)
    ↳**The Box**
      ↳ (will lead to)
        ↳**Chaos—The Wilderness**
          ↳ (where we will be helped to find)
            ↳ **The Creative and Faithful Choice**

3. One of the greatest barriers to change is fear. When we feel afraid, it is hard for us to risk and be patient. Try to identify the fears that will hold back efforts to change. What resources or support might be offered to manage that fear?

Fears   **Resources or Support**

A. My own fears

B. Leaders' fears

C. The congregation's fears

CHAPTER 5

Riding the Roller Coaster: The Emotional Cycle of Congregations in Change

We all do no end of feeling, and we mistake it for thinking.
—Mark Twain, "Corn-pone Opinions"

I had been working with the congregation for five months to help them deal with conflict between groups within the congregation and with general anger that was directed at the governing board. Both were aftermaths of the termination of the senior pastor. In the initial months of our work, most of the focus was on rebuilding relationships among members of the governing board. They were having difficulty trusting one another. Communication had broken down to the point that individuals talked openly of their concerns about other board members.

As a part of our work, we had agreed from the very beginning that there would be full communication with the whole congregation and that, at a certain time in the process, there would be an open meeting with all members of the congregation invited. The purpose of the meeting was to share with the congregation the steps we were taking, what we were learning, and what members of the congregation could personally do to help bring change to their situation.

Just weeks before the scheduled meeting with the congregation, the interim associate pastor announced her resignation in a way that once again split the board and the congregation into factions. The board members revisited their anger and their mistrust of each other. They were again caught with a few board members having some information, but not all of the board members had all the information. In some meetings immediately after the interim's resignation, they spent a good deal of time discussing what happened, what could have happened, and what should have happened. And they were very aware that the resignation of the interim associate had reactivated anger and subgroups in the congregation. Because of the work we had already done, however, the board seemed to return quickly to working with each other and taking healthy steps to address the resignation.

Nonetheless, no one was surprised that in the congregational meeting that soon followed, members spent a good deal of time focused on the feelings and misinformation the congregation had about the resignation of the interim associate. Members expressed their doubt about the leadership of the board members. They made assumptions and conclusions based on their incomplete information and their feelings about the interim associate. They spent time trying to figure out what happened, what could have happened, and what should have happened.

After forty-five minutes of this conversation, I asked for a break in the meeting. When people regathered, I invited the members of the board to reflect on the conversation that they had been listening to and to compare it to their own conversations in their most recent board meetings. Members of the board reflected on how they had expressed the same feelings, the same doubts, and had come up with exactly the same ideas about what could or should have been done. Then I asked members of the congregation to talk about how they felt knowing that they had just repeated, in detail, the work and worry their board members had already gone through. The most helpful statements made by congregational members were those about trusting the board members to do their job because "obviously we're not doing any better than they are when we talk about it."

Leaders and members were working through exactly the same feelings in order to get to open conversation and healthy decision making. As usual, leaders were simply farther ahead in the same cycle members would need to follow.

Working with congregations in change is not a dispassionate proposition. While working with goals and programs of the congregation, leaders will also be confronted with emotions. "Anxiety provokes change," writes Peter Steinke. "It prods and pushes us toward innovation or transformation." But he continues, "If, however, it reaches a certain intensity it prevents the very change it provokes."[1] In a situation of change, leaders need to measure the emotional intensity of feelings being expressed.

This, of course, includes measuring the emotional intensity of the leaders' own feelings as well. It is important for leaders to know what they and their congregation are feeling. Consultant and author William Bridges notes that many institutional changes fail because leaders pay attention to the changes they are facing but not to the transitions people must make to accommodate the changes. Transitions are described by Bridges as "the inward journey that people must make to live into and 'own' the change."[2]

One of the dilemmas of leading change in a congregation is that it naturally engages negative and angry feelings. These negative feelings develop as general anxiety begins to increase because of the awareness of change that faces the congregation. As the anxiety increases, it begins to become more focused and people are able to identify what they fear they will lose in the change. The fear prompts the basic reaction of fight or flight that has been hardwired into all of us and into groups.[3] It is a natural and normal response. As anxiety increases and begins to find focus, some people will stay to fight for or against the change and will express anger. Others will distance themselves from the congregation, either leaving quietly so as not to engage any further discomfort or leaving with parting shots such as, "This certainly isn't what I go to church (or synagogue) for!" Obviously, not only is the congregation acting out of its fears, but it prompts fear and other feelings in the leaders as well. Suddenly the whole congregation becomes reactive.

Adding to the dilemma, and to the escalating reactivity of the congregation, is the natural response of leaders who try to explain the necessary change in greater detail as a way of dealing with the fears and the reactions they are facing. The leaders' response, however, creates a classic disconnect in communication. Responding to the language of feelings being heard in the congregation by using the language of reason to explain the necessity of intended changes does not address the feelings. It is not unlike the standard parody of the American who speaks more loudly and slowly after realizing that he is talking with someone who does not understand English. Somehow we come to the conclusion that if we simply clarify and emphasize what we are saying, the person will understand, despite the fact that we are speaking the wrong language.

The more helpful response of leaders is to wonder and question what message the feelings being expressed carry for the congregation. In chapter 3 I noted how the various parts of systems are interrelated and interconnected. Consistent with that is the understanding that the emotional system is clearly a part of the whole congregation and it is interrelated and interconnected with the relational, purposeful, and structural parts of the congregation. Rather than defending or trying to avoid the feelings being expressed in the congregation, it is much more fruitful for leaders to inquire what information is being expressed in the feelings. Such an understanding can offer alternatives for what is needed from the leaders.

The Roller Coaster of Change

A helpful tool for measuring where a congregation is emotionally and for listening to the content of the members' feelings is the "roller coaster of change." Again, like the model of chaotic change in the previous chapter, this is a descriptive lens. Such a lens helps observers gather information about what a congregation (or some subgroup within the congregation) is experiencing. From such a description, leaders can then strategize an appropriate response.

The roller coaster of change is a model that identifies a natural sequence of feelings and relationships that are a part of change. It was first adapted from Ralph G. Hirschowitz by Susan Hassinger, United Methodist bishop in the Boston area.

A Game

Before you continue reading, take a few minutes to explore your own feelings during a time of change. Work either alone or with your leadership group.

1. Recall a time of great change in your life. It does not matter whether the change was positive and exciting (for example, the birth of a child) or negative and difficult (for example, a divorce or the loss of a job).

2. Begin at the point where you first received news of this change and begin to recall the feelings you experienced as you lived through the change.

3. With attention to the sequence in which you recall the feelings, list them on a sheet of newsprint.

The roller coaster of change shows a natural progression of feelings we experience in a time of change. And it also shows that the feelings we are experiencing and expressing may offer some indication of how far along we are in accepting and owning the change.

The Roller Coaster of Change

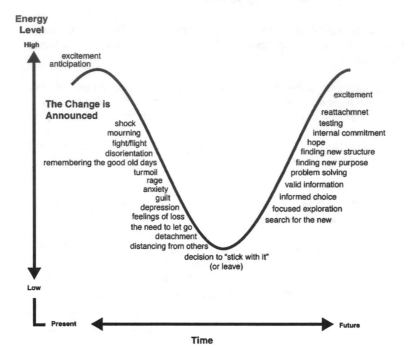

Energy Level

High

excitement
anticipation

The Change is Announced

shock
mourning
fight/flight
disorientation
remembering the good old days
turmoil
rage
anxiety
guilt
depression
feelings of loss
the need to let go
detachment
distancing from others

decision to "stick with it"
(or leave)

excitement
reattachmnet
testing
internal commitment
hope
finding new structure
finding new purpose
problem solving
valid information
informed choice
focused exploration
search for the new

Low

Present ←————————————————→ Future

Time

If you played the game above, compare your list of feelings to the roller coaster of change. Do your feelings correspond to or add to the feelings offered in the model? If you were able to identify any sequence of feelings you experienced, did they correlate with a sequence noted in the model? Of course, the model is not definitive; that is, it does not include all the feelings someone may experience in a time of change. Nor is the sequence of feelings and reactions meant to suggest that there is a clear movement from feeling to feeling in the order listed. It does, however, offer insight into the types and groupings of feelings that will be experienced, and it shows that there is a general sequence of feelings.

A number of insights about change can be gathered from this roller coaster model. Let's explore some as a way of raising helpful awareness and questions for leaders to consider.

Excitement

Notice in the roller coaster that when a change is announced, the first response may be one of increased energy and positive feelings. The line goes up. This is a fairly common experience, whether or not the news of the change is anticipated and desired. When it is first announced that a baby is expected, wife, husband, and family all feel a great amount of anticipation and celebrate with great joy. When the congregational vote is announced and there is overwhelming support to proceed with building the new facility, there is celebration. But when more difficult news is announced, people have a similar initial response. When a serious disease is finally diagnosed, the response may well be, "Thank God, we finally know what we're dealing with. Let's get going and do something about this." When the vote is taken not to extend the call or contract of a staff person, the initial response may be, "Well, we now know what we have to do. Let's get busy with a staffing study so that we can call the next staff person and get this thing going again."

There is a bit of common wisdom in family systems theory that says that as the family confronts necessary changes, the family usually gets worse before it gets better. What is suggested in the roller coaster of change is the opposite. It often seems as if the congregational system gets better before it gets worse (and then better again). That is, the initial expressions of excitement or relief allow participants to be hopeful that they will be able to march through change untouched. Leaders and members alike often become discouraged and disillusioned later as members of the congregational system begin to work through more difficult feelings. For example, clergy and music directors are dismayed at the expressions of loss and anger members eventually register about the changes in worship and music, following the initial excitement and acceptance of the need to add a new contemporary worship service to attract younger people from the community. Or leaders get upset with the number of complaints received from long-term members who talk about lack of attention and reduced programs for the older members. The leaders are upset because they can recall the support these same members initially gave to the new program and staffing priorities directed to youth when the retired visitation pastor moved to another community.

It is not uncommon for leaders and members to have a sense of betrayal or disappointment that things did not go smoothly after the initial response of people pulling together and the excitement of people wanting to see changes implemented. It is helpful and healthy for leaders to be aware of the positive energy that often begins the cycle of change. And leaders need to know that these positive feelings are naturally followed by more difficult feelings and a loss of energy. This information allows leaders to avoid feeling blindsided by the criticisms they will experience from the very same people who initially offered support and expressed relief. Leaders can then interpret the changes in congregational attitudes to members who remember the initial enthusiasm and begin to worry that "we're losing support" as the more difficult feelings begin to be expressed.

Significantly, leaders can depersonalize the criticisms and concerns they will hear. To be aware that initial enthusiasm will run a natural cycle through some level of anger and depression helps leaders be less personally sensitive to criticisms that will be leveled at them. And such awareness may help to alleviate some worry about having personally failed at leading the congregation in change.

In the discussion of systems theory in chapter 3, I explained that systems (such as congregations) naturally seek balance or equilibrium. And I noted that this search for equilibrium is often experienced by leaders as resistance to the change they are seeking. In fact, as the cycle of feelings in the congregation runs from enthusiasm to anger or depression, many leaders interpret the shift as evidence of personal criticism from members or other leaders. Rather, the shift may be the natural workings of a healthy system seeking stability. Changing systems balance and stabilize themselves by using positive and negative feedback loops.[4]

Feedback loops are the bits of information within the system, or congregation, that are used to keep internal fluctuations within acceptable and sustainable norms. "Positive" and "negative" as descriptors of feedback loops are not evaluative terms. They do not mean "good" and "bad" feedback loops. Rather a "positive" feedback loop is an "excitor." It tells the system that it is too calm. It is like an alarm clock that tells you that you are too calm and inactive when you sleep and it is time to be up and moving. So it gives you positive, that is, stimulating, information. It is like the initial enthusiasm the congregation offers in response to an announced change that suggests, "Let's get going!" In contrast, a "negative" feedback loop is information that is introduced into the system to slow it down. It inhibits the change and acts like a speeding ticket. The most common response we have after receiving a speeding ticket is to slow down and to be very conscious of our speed. Similarly, the initial enthusiasm in the congregation about change will often be followed with more difficult feelings that will act as speeding tickets, that is, negative information that will slow the change down and try to restore a feeling of stability. By using both positive and negative feedback loops, the congregational system will try to keep itself intact and healthy as it rides the roller coaster of change.

An easy example of this is the rather common experience of tickling a baby. When you initially start to pay attention to the baby and tickle him or her, the baby laughs and giggles in response. The laughter is a positive feedback loop. The baby's response gives you encouraging information that the play is pleasurable and that the baby wants you to continue. The laughter "excites" your participation in the play, and you continue to tickle and perhaps to laugh yourself. When the baby is over-stimulated by your play, however, he or she will begin to cry. The tickling pleasure has reached its upper limit and is now being experienced as discomfort, and the baby immediately offers a negative feedback loop by crying. This clearly tells you to slow down. Our most natural instinct at that point is to hug and cuddle the baby to help him reestablish a feeling of comfort and stability. In most cases the crying is not intentional resistance to your tickling, and it is not evidence that you have been bad or done something wrong by stimulating the baby. It is not information you necessarily need to personalize. But it is information. It tells you what the baby is experiencing and what the baby needs from you next. The emotional cycle of the congregation as it moves from excitement through depression and on provides, similarly, information. It is important for leaders to identify how they are feeling and how others in the congregation are feeling to help them know what the congregation needs from them next.

The Feelings

In his work with transitions Bridges describes the process of change as involving three phases:

1. letting go of the old
2. an empty or fallow time in between
3. a beginning

He writes, "Growing frightened, we are likely to try to abort the three-phase process of ending, lostness, and beginnings. We even twist this pattern around so that beginnings come first, then endings, and then … then what? Nothing. It is when we turn things around in that way that transitions become so unintelligible and frightening."[5] When thinking of change, people naturally want to start with the new beginning. This anxious desire to begin the change is consistent with the "let's get going" feeling that is so often expressed at the initiation of change. It is the desire to move ahead and fix the problem without wanting to slow down to deal with the difficulties along the way. In large part, it is the wish not to deal with the need to let go of old ways or to live through the confusion of the chaos that feels so unproductive.

Yet the fact is that in order to make the transition into the new goals or plans of the congregation, people first need to do the work of letting go of what has been. This then often ushers people into the wilderness described in the model of chaos in the preceding chapter. It is during these stages that a host of feelings make themselves known such as shock, mourning, disorientation, turmoil, guilt, depression—as indicated on the roller coaster of change.

Words such as these—"shock," "mourning," "disorientation," and others listed on the down slope of the roller coaster—sound rather dire. At this point as a leader of change, you may be asking yourself, "Oh Lord, what have I let myself in for?" In many congregations, however, these feelings are expressed along a continuum of intensity. Although in some cases the feeling of "shock" may be reported full strength in its own "shocking" way, often the feeling will be offered in a milder form. A friend and former colleague of mine was surprised to learn that he was perceived as a "complainer" in his work group. "Me?" he replied. "I never complain." Yet he had a habit of receiving information that he was not expecting or not wanting by responding with an expression such as "Oh my gracious!" It was a complaint and his coworkers recognized it as such. But like him, his complaint was gracious. Leading change requires leaders to recognize the feelings and the information being offered by the congregation, be it gracious or gross. And to recognize the legitimacy of these feelings allows leaders to search for responsible ways to respond to them.

In chapter 3 on systems theory, the term "holon" was offered to describe the interplay between the parts and the whole of a system. This suggests one can often understand what is happening in the larger system by paying attention to the lower level, which will reflect the same or similar issues as those being experienced in the whole. Leaders need to pay attention to what they themselves are feeling in order to understand what feelings the congregation may need to address as a way of working through change.

Following is a chart of the eight stages of change that an individual will go through in order to participate with the change process in a healthy way. It was developed by Susan Campbell, a psychologist specializing in organizational change who consults with corporations managing the large changes they now face as organizations and their employees face as individuals. It is helpful to pay attention to the tasks that need to be addressed at each level, the skills that need to be developed and used, what needs to be let go, and what needs to be learned. With an understanding of holon, it is appropriate to extrapolate these descriptions about individuals to the whole congregation, which will go through these stages with similar needs and demands. Note the high degree of overlap between this model of eight stages of change for the individual with the roller coaster of change for congregations.

The Eight Stages of Change

	Stage 1: Feeling Unsettled	Stage 2: Denying/ Resisting	Stage 3: Facing the Present Situation	Stage 4: Letting Go into the Unknown	Stage 5: Envisioning the Desired Future	Stage 6: Exploring New Options	Stage 7: Committing to Action	Stage 8: Integrating the Change
Task:	allow myself to feel unsettled; admit dissatisfaction	recognize my resistance or denial for what it is	face my situation realistically; see what it is	grieve the issues associated with saying goodbye, including what I lost by hanging on too long to an inappropriate situation	visualize what I want or how I want to be in the future	explorations of the new options I have envisioned for myself; experimenting with new behaviors and feelings	commit to action; choose the options that seem most appropriate	integrating the new quality/ behavior into the rest of my life so that I operate at a higher level of complexity and maturity
Skills:	ability to feel unpleasant feelings	ability to overcome or manage my fears	nonjudgmental, nonblaming attitude	ability to feel sadness, ability to tolerate uncertainty	ability to feel wants	ability to take risks	ability to make decisions and eliminate options	ability to feel and act on more than one impulse at once
Let Go:	my attachment to always feeling fine or in control	my denial or resistance	old picture of who I am or how things should be	the need to know what I want and where I'm going	safety of sticking with what is familiar	having to be good at everything	other alternatives; the need to keep all options open	the sense of loss associated with choosing this instead of that
Learn:	I can handle pain/discomfort.	I understand how my denial/ resistance is an attempt to protect myself.	I can move ahead into the unknown without triggering more denial/ resistance.	I can handle not knowing where I'm heading or how things will turn out.	I trust that something new and more appropriate emerges out of the chaos.	I am open to new ways of being and doing things.	I can envision something new and make it a reality.	I can continue to learn and grow.

The Appropriate Leadership Response

Throughout this book I have been saying that leading change in the congregation requires leaders to respond *appropriately* to the needs of the congregation. This is much more critical than knowing the answer to the questions or problems, or being able to fix the perceived problems of the congregation. The issue of "appropriate leadership response" can be seen most clearly in this roller coaster model. Are leaders doing what the congregation needs?

If you draw a vertical line through the center of the roller coaster model there are two distinct halves. On the left half of the model are the more difficult feelings often expressed and experienced as negatives and problems in change. Also on this left side is the task of letting go. On the right side of the model are the feelings of hope and the actions of gathering valid information, beginning problem solving, and a reforming of the congregation in response to the change. These are often expressed and experienced as positives.

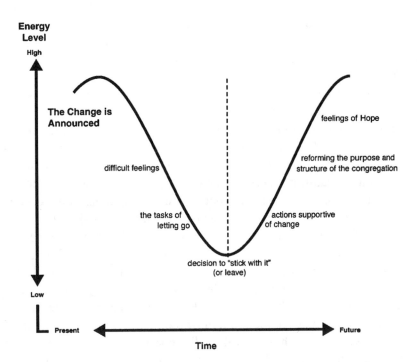

When congregation leaders try to respond appropriately to the congregation, they need to be sure they are talking to the correct half. Our tendency to always speak from the right side of the roller coaster perhaps results from our society's focus on being persuasive. **It is easier to persuade by being positive.** Stephen Covey, president of the Covey Leadership Center and the nonprofit Institute for Principle-Centered Leadership, points out that our culture values communication highly and that from our earliest moments we are trained and educated to communicate. Most of our training, however, is about how to transmit messages (both orally and in writing), and we receive very little training about how to listen.[7] As a matter of fact, much of our communication is a form of debate. We listen to another person only long enough to figure out what we want to say next in response. We tend to be rewarded for making points clearly and convincingly by winning over the objections or counterpoints offered by the "other side." This cultural pattern is especially true of our leaders. Communication by leaders is most often perceived as a matter of persuading. Although Speed Leas identifies six different styles of working with conflict, not surprisingly he identifies persuading as "... the most frequently used of all the conflict management strategies. (Indeed, it is the most frequently misused strategy.)"[8]

Because we are concerned about being persuasive and think the role of leader is to be able to convince people to do what is necessary, we often respond inappropriately. Leaders in congregations quite often tend to hear the feelings and issues on the *left half of the roller coaster* and respond by talking to people (persuading) about the hopes and the actions on the *right half of the roller coaster*. For example, in the midst of discussions about the new informal worship service that will replace the eleven o'clock traditional service, the chairperson of the worship committee suddenly is inundated with concerns and complaints from "eleven o'clockers." They complain about destroying "their" worship, taking away "their" service, making them lose contact with the people they have always worshipped with, and so forth. These are left-half concerns. These are the feelings of loss and of anger that need to be acknowledged and addressed in order to help people move toward accepting change.

Characteristically, the response of leaders is to answer those complaints and concerns from the left half of the model by talking about the ideas that live on the right side of the roller coaster. Patiently (she hopes) the chairperson of the worship committee explains one more time why it is important to have a contemporary worship service. She explains that people new to the church respond much more easily to contemporary music and are unfamiliar with European classical forms of music that go with traditional worship. She explains that young people are comfortable in informal settings and that the formality of the traditional liturgy is confusing and uncomfortable to them. She reminds them of the goals set by the board to increase membership and to attract younger people to the congregation. And she explains why the leaders hope the new informal service will help meet that goal.

In other words, when presented with the feelings from the left half of the roller coaster, the chairperson does what many (most?) leaders characteristically do: She responds with the reasons, explanations, and hopes from the right side of the roller coaster. The language of the left side of the roller coaster is the language of feelings, and the language of the right side of the roller coaster tends to be reason and logic. "If only we could get people to *understand*," sigh the leaders. But often people are not dealing with understanding, they are dealing with feelings.

Look again at the first four stages of change, which Campbell says need to be managed by people in order to cope with change (page 116). They include being able to let go of attachment to always feeling in control, being able to handle the discomfort and uncertainty of what the change will mean, being able to overcome and manage fears, letting go of the old picture of the way things should be, and so forth. On the left side of the roller coaster people tend to talk the language of feelings.

Not being aware of the disconnect, it is common for leaders to take extra efforts to explain and clarify the reasons and goals prompting the change, to redouble their efforts to be persuasive. We are now back to the caricature I offered at the beginning of the chapter about the American who uses the funny but failing strategy of speaking more slowly and loudly when confronted with someone who does not speak English. Responding to feelings by speaking reasons more slowly and clearly does not work. Trying to pull people from the left side to the right side of the roller coaster is a persuasive strategy. And this *does* engender resistance from people. The insight that fits this scenario is that people do not resist change. They resist being changed.

When dealing with the left side of the roller coaster, it is more important for leaders to listen (and to demonstrate that they have listened) than it is for them to talk. Stephen Covey notes that "empathic commu-

nication," communication that rests on listening to and understanding
the other, is one of the central habits of effective people. He summarizes
this habit as: "Seek first to understand, then to be understood."[9] Covey
recognizes that one of the best tools for negotiating is listening, not talking. It is the leader who has done the hard work of listening to the concerns of the other who will then be listened to. Empathic communication
follows the principle of satisfied needs. As Covey writes:

> If all the air were suddenly sucked out of the room you're in right
> now, what would happen to your interest in this book? You wouldn't
> care about the book; you wouldn't care about anything except get-
> ting air. Survival would be your only motivation.
>
> But now that you have air, it doesn't motivate you. This is one
> of the greatest insights in the field of human motivation: *Satisfied
> needs do not motivate.* It's only the unsatisfied need that motivates.
>
> Next to physical survival, the greatest need of a human being is
> psychological survival—to be understood, to be affirmed, to be vali-
> dated, to be appreciated.[10]

Leaders and members who are on the left half of the roller coaster
need to be listened to, not convinced.

A commitment to listen to others, then, prompts one of the most important lessons leaders need to keep in mind. And that is that listening
to others does *not* require that you agree with them. One of the reasons
we often avoid truly listening to the concerns or complaints of others is
that we suspect or know that we will not agree with them and will be
placed in a position of having to agree in order to move ahead or keep
our relationship. This invites leaders to use the strategy, "Don't ask the
question if you can't handle the answer." We avoid asking people how
they are feeling about the proposed change because they might tell us.

Listening is listening. It is not agreement. Listening means being
able to be clear about the concerns people are raising and being able to
demonstrate that the concerns have been heard, considered, and perhaps
resolved. In one congregation I was continuously interrupted by one man
who insisted that I and the denominational executive had not listened to
his concerns. On the third or fourth interruption suggesting that he had
not been listened to, I paused to recount the number of times and ways
his concerns had been heard. I mentioned the copies of letters I had in

my file from the denominational executive addressing his concerns, the number of meetings the executive had convened and attended, the number of meetings I had led, and the report I had developed that clearly included his concerns. I ended by asking him to consider that the issue was not that he had not been listened to but that he did not agree with the response he had received to his concerns. He paused and then said, "Oh, I guess you're right." From that point on he became an active participant in the process I was leading to deal with the changes his congregation was facing.

Helping people feel listened to is not necessarily so uncomfortable or confrontative. It means demonstrating to others that their concerns have been heard and included in the planning. For example, one small congregation had identified a team of six people who would do planning for them. The team of six quickly learned they would need to consider some rather large changes, which might include major shifts in program emphasis and possibly major renovations to their current building or relocation to another. Before they got to the stage of writing a report and offering recommendations to the congregation, they offered a time of listening. They invited everyone in the congregation to an all-day meeting. As a major part of that meeting, the planning team shared with the congregation what they had learned in their work as a planning team and that they realized they faced the possibility of large changes. The team gave the members plenty of time to discuss their work and their learnings. And then they asked people to share their enthusiasm for what they had heard from the planning team as well as any concerns they wanted the planning team to take into consideration. About fifteen concerns were listed on newsprint. Before the members of the congregation left that day, they were invited to use a marker to make checks indicating on the newsprint the three concerns that were most critical to them personally. When completing their work and writing the report the planning team gave special attention to these concerns. And they were clear in their report about how they had addressed these critical concerns from the congregation in their recommendations. All of the members were not pleased and in full agreement with the recommendations. But having their concerns treated openly and seriously was very helpful to many of the members as they faced the changes ahead.

I am always amazed at the number of instances in which governing boards receive letters or messages of complaints and put the concern on the agenda, discuss it, and even take action on it, but never respond to the person(s) who initiated the concern. A person who sends a letter outlining a concern should receive a letter that describes the way the board dealt with the concern and what the outcome will be. A person who gives a message to a board member asking him or her to raise a concern with the board needs to receive a personal message explaining when and how the board dealt with the concern. It is all right for the board not to satisfy the concern or complaint. After all, the responsibility of the board is to make faithful and critical decisions for the ministry of the whole congregation, not to try to find compromises that will address most of the complaints and keep most of the members happy. But it is not all right for boards or leaders not to respond to concerns or to act silently without offering information about the response to the people who hold the concerns. The left half of the roller coaster is the feeling side, and it needs to be addressed with responses that honor those feelings.

Similarly, it is important for leaders to pay attention to the worship and study life of the congregation in times of change. If the congregation is on the left half of the roller coaster and experiencing the deeper feelings that accompany change, it does not help for the preacher to preach about the promised land and how good it will be to arrive. It will be much more helpful to spend preaching or teaching time in the wilderness, to allow members to explore what it means for a community to be faithful on the way to the destination of great change. I take Walter Brueggemann's statement quite seriously when he claims that "the Old Testament stories of exile might be a resource, perhaps the only resource, to move us from denial and despair to possibility."[11]

Brueggemann notes that in response to the displacement of the exile, Leviticus offered clear guidelines for behavior according to the notions of holiness. He points out that these "displaced people for whom almost everything was out of control set out to reorder and recover life through an intentional resolve about communion with God." From Deuteronomy Brueggemann suggests that we can learn how the Israelites worked to establish a sense of community in exile. He writes, "Dislocation carries with it the temptation to be preoccupied with self, to flee the hard task of community formation for the sake of private well-being." In Deuteronomy the Israelites worked to strengthen their community as a way of moving beyond despair.

Leviticus and Deuteronomy do not rank high on most of our lists of engaging and exciting books to study. And certainly, apart from Brueggemann's suggestion, there may be other places in Scripture where your congregation may find helpful words for a time of change. But Brueggemann raises the question of what is being preached, taught, and sung in congregational gatherings in times of change. If your congregation is on the left half of the roller coaster and you are preaching or teaching from the right half, the words will sound hollow to the listeners and people will feel manipulated into change. If people in the congregation are on the left half of the roller coaster and feeling displaced, however, working with Leviticus may be very helpful. If the congregation can sense that the Holiness Code was developed in an effort to reestablish some stability in a time when Israel felt out of control, it can help to raise the question, How will the congregation agree to live together in a time when they feel out of control?

The Point of Decision

At the very bottom of the roller coaster of change is a point of decision, not a feeling. The decision is whether to stick with it (or leave). It is important to notice that the turning point on the roller coaster of change is a rational decision, not a resolution of all the feelings. The purpose of appropriate leadership is not to care for all the feelings people have, or to resolve all concerns so members move ahead with the changes in complete unanimity and satisfaction. Rather, leadership needs to help hold people in their feelings and to address their concerns so people can be brought to a point where they will decide. Will they stay with this congregation in a time of change? Or will they separate from the congregation? In which direction do they *choose* to move?

In today's culture, which in many ways honors differences and diversity, it is unreasonable to assume that decisions or new directions in a congregation will accommodate and please everyone. Indeed, two of the critical things leaders themselves need to let go of in a time of change are their desire to make decisions that will please everyone and their memory of a time when that seemed possible.

What the roller coaster of change helps us recognize is that when people make the rational decision to commit to the change, they are prepared to enter the work of the right half of the roller coaster. It is in this half that they need to gather their energy again and begin to focus their efforts to accomplish the change before them. During this phase, people do need accurate information, and leaders need to educate the congregation about the change that is the goal of the ministry. People need to know what will be different and how the congregation will be faithful, so people will know clearly what they have committed themselves to and what they are working for. In Campbell's eight stages of change, this is the work of envisioning the new future, exploring new options, committing to action, and integrating the change into the practice of the congregation. Indeed, once the congregation has made the decision to stick with it, it is time for leaders to begin to talk again and be persuasive.

Where Is the Congregation on the Roller Coaster of Change?

Using the roller coaster of change as a lens through which to view and understand the congregation offers leaders the opportunity to ask, Where is my congregation on this roller coaster? As I observed earlier, this allows leaders to consider what the congregation needs from them in order to move through the various stages and experiences of change.

The dilemma is that in most congregations it is easy to find individuals at almost every point on the roller coaster. Some people will still be experiencing the initial enthusiasm at the same time as others are experiencing deep feelings about the change, and others are struggling to decide whether the change is right for them, when still others are already at work trying to make the change happen. In fact, as a pastor to congregations that went through periods of great change, I am very aware that I myself might be anywhere on the roller coaster depending upon which day you ask. On my worst days I was like the weather in England: If you do not like the way it is, wait an hour and it will change.

On the one hand it is very important to know where you yourself are on the roller coaster of change if you are a leader in a congregation. As a person responsible to lead change, to make decisions for the good of the whole, and to respond appropriately to the needs of others, it is important not to be constrained by your own needs and place on the roller coaster. On the other hand, however, it is also important to have a sense of where the critical mass of the congregation is because it is impossible to meet everyone's needs at all times.

In most cases locating "most of the people" in the congregation on the roller coaster is not a simple and measurable task. It is not easy to get clear data that will tell you where the critical mass might be at any moment. Leaders tend to know intuitively, however, and are remarkably accurate in identifying where the congregation is and what parts need to move ahead. I will often sketch the roller coaster on newsprint and talk through its various points with a group of congregational leaders. I then ask each of the leaders to decide individually where they believe the critical mass of the congregation could be placed on the roller coaster of change. I invite them to think of their experiences with members of the congregation to help them decide. What kind of messages have they been hearing from the congregation? How much energy do people have for their congregation? What kinds of questions do people ask them as leaders? Then having decided individually, I invite each leader to put a mark on the curve to show where they think the congregation is in the process of change.

There is usually a strong consensus about which section of the roller coaster the greater mass of the congregation is experiencing at any given time. In fact, if several critical masses in the congregation are at different places on the roller coaster, leaders intuitively know and will place them on the model. Doing such an exercise allows leaders to move quickly into conversations about what the congregation needs at that moment to help manage the change. The exercise also helps leaders to recognize when their efforts are being slowed down by just a few individuals or a small group. In some cases this helps leaders to understand how they might respond to the small groups to offer support. Or it may help the leaders to recognize that they do not need to be held back by the one or two vocal people who consistently present all the concerns and fears that seem to be blocking the change.

In fact, if you are wondering where your congregation or individuals in your congregation may be on the roller coaster of change, the best way to find out is to ask. The roller coaster is a very simple lens, easily understood and consistent with people's experience of change. It is easy to invite people to talk about what they are experiencing by locating themselves on the roller coaster. The very act of using the model to enable people to talk about their experience can support the effort to change.

For example, I was invited to work with the national board of one denomination whose representatives were feeling worn and wearied by the changes they were experiencing. The invitation to work with them was prompted by the considerable amount of complaining and the feelings of helplessness they had become aware of in their conversations with one another. They were clear with me that I was not expected to help them work toward solutions to their problems, which they recognized as being long-term and difficult. They did, however, want help in talking about the complaints and their feelings. After making the necessary introductions and stating the purpose for our work together, I introduced the roller coaster of change with their help. It was easily done in twenty minutes and people indicated they believed they understood it. I then asked each person to consider his or her own relationship to the issues this board was facing and gave them several minutes to consider where they would place themselves on the roller coaster. Finally, I asked them to use the marker and locate themselves on the model, without regard to where others might place themselves.

The group was fascinated by the results. Although they had been very sensitive to the amount of complaining they heard in their own conversations (suggesting they were on the left half of the model and dealing with feelings), over 85 percent of the group members placed themselves well into the right half of the model. Individually they saw themselves as working on the upswing of the change facing them. We laughed and joked about people not telling the truth when they placed their mark on the roller coaster. But I asked them to break into small groups and to work to explain the results we had in the self-reported marks on the roller coaster.

By the end of the afternoon the consensus of the group was that despite the complaining they all seemed to do, it was clear that most of the board members had made the decision to stick with it and were actively busy trying to do something about it. The conclusion of the group was that it was now time to stop spending their time complaining to one another about what was happening and to begin sharing with each other the efforts by which they were each trying to address the changes.

Leaders Precede Members

It is also helpful for leaders to recognize that typically they precede members on the roller coaster ride through change. Leaders experience the excitement of the start and all the accompanying feelings sooner than the members of the congregation because the responsibility of leaders requires that they deal with the questions and issues first. Leaders tend to reach the decision point prior to the members and begin the right half climb sooner than the members.

In fact, one of the issues for leaders is to remember that members are not sharing the experience of change at the same rate as they and are not usually dealing with the same feelings and ideas as the leaders. Commonly the leaders are already consolidating plans on the right half of the roller coaster while members are feeling stuck with the difficult feelings of the left half.

This difference in timing between leaders and members can be problematic. Leaders can feel frustrated and unsupported by the members who are still complaining and not pitching in to help. Members can feel disconnected from leaders who are busy planning the work of change and who seem insensitive to their concerns. Leaders often need to be reminded that they need to reach back and help members through the same steps of learning and coping with feelings that they have had to work their way through. The case study at the beginning of this chapter is an example of leaders needing to reach back to support the members through the same questions, doubts, and feelings they have already experienced. Similarly, it is helpful for members to know that the leaders have preceded them through the same steps. Continual communication between the groups that stresses the steps and stages they have experienced in common is important in order to keep these two subgroups from being adversaries as they hold different positions through the stages of change.

Leaders' Need to Care for Themselves

The final learning that comes from watching congregations going through the roller coaster of change is that leaders will need to care for themselves. This is particularly true for clergy and for other individuals who are highly visible in the organizational structure of the congregation. The dilemma is that leaders experience the same feelings and same reactions as do the members facing issues of change. As noted above, leaders simply tend to cycle through the feelings and reactions before other members do. Leaders are also responsible, however, for addressing the feelings and reactions of others in the congregation.

It is often not helpful for the pastor or key leaders to share with the whole congregation their doubts, bumps, and bruises about issues of change, or the anger they have received from others because of the change. The anger and depression some members feel in their congregation at a time of change may well be focused on the clergyperson or a key lay leader, who then feels the bruise of their accusation. The pain or discomfort of the change actually belongs to the community, but it does not help to tell people about it. Instead of helping, talking about the bruises often engenders anger or guilt, expressed as "Look what we've done" to our clergy or our board president (or "Look what they are accusing us of doing to them!")

Many congregations value openly sharing personal needs among members as a way of offering support either in prayer or in action. People are encouraged to be forthright about problems they are encountering or illnesses they are experiencing. In such situations I encourage congregational leaders to try to distinguish which pains and problems belong to them personally and which are theirs "professionally" because of their leadership role. In other words, if their son has just been in an automobile accident, it would be important to tell the congregation. This is a personally difficult experience members will want to know about. People in the congregation will want to support the leader and the son through prayer or through offers of meals, transportation to the hospital or other actions.

If the pain is experienced, however, because members in the congregation have complained about their leadership or there are rumors circulating that question their ability to lead, this is not helpful information to feed back to the congregation with the hope that members will offer support. This is pain that is connected to their professional or leadership role in the congregation. It is closely related to the experience of change the congregation is going through. This is the pain central leaders in congregations need to care for outside of the congregational system, which is not equipped to address or help with it. Taking pain "outside the congregation" means talking with someone like a spiritual director, a trusted colleague, a therapist, or a confidential support group (not with one's spouse, who is also a part of the congregational system). Clergy and key leaders need to take these bruises to other trusted people so they can help themselves by dealing with the feelings responsibly.

Exercises for Leaders

The following diagnostic conversations will help you identify intuitively where your congregation may be in the process of change and what is needed from leaders. Invite leaders to use their own experience and information to test whether there is agreement about what the congregation is facing.

Questions about " members" refer to the "critical mass" of the people in the congregation. It is common to find an individual who sits at every point or stage in descriptive models such as these. It is not particularly helpful to identify where specific individuals are unless there is a need to help certain individuals move past a stage where they have become active blockers of change. It is usually more helpful for leaders to try to describe where most of the people in the congregation are (the critical mass) as a way of knowing what the congregation needs from leaders.

1. Using the following model of the roller coaster of change, invite leaders to indicate their intuitive assessment of where the two groups are at the present moment: members and leaders. Invite the leaders also to identify where they would place themselves individually on the roller coaster of change. In making their assessment they should consider their own experience. Questions to help them focus their experience include:

- What kinds of messages have leaders been hearing?
- How much energy do people have for their congregation?
- What kinds of questions do people ask leaders?

When all participants have made their own individual assessment, invite them to mark a single copy of the roller coaster of change as indicated below. It is not important to identify who made which marks. It is more helpful for the full group of leaders to look at the overall pattern of responses that develops from this exercise.
Use these codes:

M—Members of the congregation are here on the roller coaster of change.
L—Leaders of the congregation *as a group* are here on the roller coaster of change.
I—I as an individual leader put myself here on the roller coaster of change.

2. Use these questions for discussion:

- Is there a pattern in the responses?
- What does this suggest the congregation needs from leaders?
- What does this suggest leaders need in this time of change?
- What does this suggest I need in this time of change?
- Are there any identifiable subgroups in the congregation that suggest we need to address more than one stage of change in the congregation?
- (What other questions occur to you when looking at your pattern?)

The Roller Coaster of Change

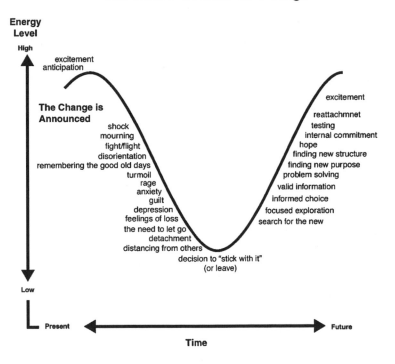

CHAPTER 6

Spinning Wheels Gather No Traction: Congregational Preferences in Change

Finding the Right Way

> Two Jesuit priests both wanted a cigarette while they prayed. They decided to ask their bishop for permission. The first asked but was told no. A little while later he spotted his friend smoking. "Why did the bishop allow you to smoke and not me?" he asked. "Because you asked if you could smoke while you prayed and I asked if I could pray while I smoked!" the friend replied.

"But what are we actually going to do?" asked a rather frustrated member of the board. "I'm an action person, and this talk about vision and setting priorities isn't solving our problems," she concluded.

I had been asked by these leaders to work with them several times over a period of a few years to help them with strategic planning and setting directions for their ministry. What was unique about this center-city, "tall steeple" congregation was its commitment to diversity and inclusion in an urban cultural environment that worked hard to separate and exclude people. The congregation (and to a somewhat lesser degree the leadership group itself) was broad and inclusive of a wide range of people who in other settings naturally lived and worked apart. There were African Americans, Native Americans, liberals and conservatives, traditionalists and contemporaries, wealthy and poor. In fact, there was a wide range of nationalities represented in the congregation. There were gays and straights, healthy and ill members. The diversity within this congregation was amazing and the congregational lifestyle reflected it. Worship included traditional European

hymns, Native American dance, Dixieland jazz, praise choruses, and
Gospel anthems. The members' interests and involvements in mission
were equally broad.

But I had returned to work with these leaders for several evenings
because once again they were feeling uncomfortable and unsure about
what to do next and which direction to follow. Theirs was a congrega-
tion so diverse that doing anything would displease some people and
never be enough for others. What they were searching for was their
center. What was it that held them together? And once found (or more
accurately, once found again during this most recent period of ques-
tioning), how could that center be used to set appropriate goals and
establish priorities for using resources? The small leadership group
was tired from meeting diverse needs and trying to reestablish their vi-
sion as a source of energy and direction.

At a rather critical moment in the conversation the frustrated
board member pushed her question pointedly. "But what are we actu-
ally going to do?"

Rolling stones gather no moss. Everyone knows this old adage,
which encourages action and reminds us of the benefits of constant work
and movement. But I would like to offer the counterpoint: "Spinning
wheels gather no traction." There are times when we need to be more
discerning and more strategic in our responses and when the quick move
to action will consume a good amount of energy but will produce few, if —
any, results. As the little story about the Jesuit priests at the beginning
of the chapter suggests, it may be more productive to ask the right question or to find the right approach than to swing into action and try to
change things.

In fact, the propensity to action, to "spin wheels," can be a subtle
and collusive trap that is actually designed to subvert any real change.
This can be seen in the distinction between "restructuring" and "revisioning" in congregations. To understand that distinction, let's look at
the life cycle of a congregation.

Life Cycle of Congregations

In a wonderfully descriptive model, Robert Dale describes separate and distinct stages in the life cycle of a congregation that are much like the steps and stages we might think of in our own human life cycle.[1] That is, there are distinct developmental stages in the life of a congregation, much as there are in our individual lives, and each stage has its own discrete tasks and characteristics that parallel the individual's. For us the use of stage-of-life descriptions such as infant, toddler, child, adolescent, young adult, and so on instantly identifies separate phases of life, each of which has characteristics, skills, and goals distinct from the others. Similarly, suggests Dale, congregations go through stages in their own life cycles that follow the pattern below:

The Life Cycle of a Congregation

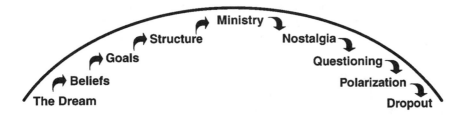

Let's briefly walk through the various stages. The DREAM is the vision of what could be or a statement about what God calls the congregation to be. The dream, or vision, is the source of energy and direction that fuels the ministry. It may be a dream to found a new congregation where there is none to serve a particular community. Or it may be a dream to specialize in serving mentally handicapped children. The dream gives the congregation a clear identity and purpose.

It is followed by the stage of BELIEFS, which is where the congregation begins to build the critical mass of people who will live out the dream. In this stage people who share a common belief system gather. These folk hold in common both the way in which faith is shared in the tradition and practice of the congregation, and the specific dream this one congregation has committed itself to. In a time in which differences

are honored and congregations need to address the specific needs and
wants of individual members, the stage of beliefs is critical. This is the
point at which congregations need to be very clear about what is distinc-
tive about themselves and what specifically and uniquely they are committed to do or provide in ministry. It is a way of calling to the congregation people who can share the belief.

The stages of GOALS and STRUCTURE are the stages most familiar to and most understood by congregational members. These are the
organizational stages in which the dream is broken into recognizable
and achievable steps by setting goals and providing the necessary structure (committees, timetables, resources of dollars and people, and programs). These are favored stages by North American congregations,
which are well practiced in the problem-solving model that was described earlier in this book. And these are the stages where we do our
problem solving. They are the high-energy stages when people put their
efforts together to achieve the dream.

When the stages of goal setting and structure are handled well, the
stage of MINISTRY naturally follows. It is important to recognize that
the stage of ministry is the accomplishment or the fulfillment of the
dream. In fact, when the stage of ministry is reached it signals that the
dream is complete and is being lived out. If the dream was to build a
new facility for a new congregation, the stage of ministry is reached
when the facility is complete and the new congregation is worshipping
there. If the dream is to be a congregation that is called to care for mentally handicapped children, the stage of ministry is reached when the series of monthly birthday parties for the children begins and the children
and their families begin to show up for worship, using the specially designed room attached to the sanctuary.

When the stage of ministry is reached, the goal is accomplished.
The energy needed to get the congregation to this stage of an accomplished dream has been expended and people naturally want to rest a
bit and enjoy goals accomplished. It is the feeling the disciples had after
the transfiguration of Christ (Matthew 17:1-13). Peter and James were
on the mountaintop with Jesus as he was transfigured before them and
joined by Moses and Elijah, who spoke with him. In the experience of
the disciples, it was a high moment indeed! Peter's response was, "Lord,
it is good for us to be here; if you wish, I will make three dwellings here
…" (v. 4). The temptation when the mountaintop of ministry is reached

is to want to make it last and to honor it. Like Peter, members proclaim that it is good to be here and they want to remain. For members the time of ministry is a time of high satisfaction. And in moments of satisfaction, there is little motivation to make changes and to move on.

Congregations cannot remain in the stage of ministry without change, however. The internal environment of the congregation changes as people get older and some members move away to be replaced by new members with different needs. The external environment also changes both locally and in the broader culture. The end result is that congregations cannot sustain ministry by committing to the status quo. And if they do not intentionally change to meet the new needs by continually reframing their stage of ministry, they will enter into the next stage of the life cycle.

NOSTALGIA is the time of remembering. This is when members recall the stories of the time when the congregation was at the height of its ministry. "Remember how we used to have to put up extra seats in the sanctuary on Christmas Eve?" they say. Or, "Remember when we used to have thirty-five kids in our youth program?"

If not interrupted in the stage of nostalgia, congregations move on to the stage of QUESTIONING in which memories are turned into clear questions about the present. They now begin to ask, "Why don't we have to put up extra chairs in the sanctuary on Christmas Eve any longer?" And, "Why don't we have thirty-five kids in our youth program any more?" The stage of questioning often moves quickly to the stage of PO-LARIZATION as people answer the questions. "I'll tell you why," comes the response. "We don't have to put up extra chairs on Christmas Eve any more because of the preacher. If he preached a decent sermon, the people would come out!" In the stage of polarization, it is important to understand that the answers to the questions that started in nostalgia do not have to be right. They simply need to be offered. Members will then begin to polarize and form subgroups depending upon whether they agree with the answer or not. Uninterrupted, the stage of polarization leads to DROPOUT, and the congregation is potentially facing its end.

The sequence Dale offers is simple and easy for most members to understand from their own experience. And although most congregations tend to have rather long life cycles that extend well beyond the lifetime of the individual, it is not difficult for most members to know intuitively which stage their congregation is currently experiencing. Of course, the sequence of stages can be, and usually is, repeated a number of times in the history of a congregation as it moves from one dream/vision to a new one that will address the next chapter of its history.

And the shift to the new dream or vision is the key. I noted earlier that if the sequence of stages following the stage of ministry is not interrupted, it will continue in a disabling way. Leaders do want to interrupt the downward cycle of stages that come after ministry. And there are essentially two ways they can work do that: *revisioning* or *restructuring*.

Revisioning and Restructuring

Revisioning is asking, What does God call us to next? What is the next chapter in our congregational life history supposed to look like, and how do we get there? These are questions at the foundation of a new dream or a different vision. And the new dream carries with it the energy and the direction to start a new cycle in the history of the congregation with new enthusiasms and commitments. A congregation that once had a vision of participating in global missions through their dollar support of foreign mission programs may have accomplished their goals in ministry. But the energy may also be running low as dollars have tightened over the years and members no longer feel the connection with missions. This always happens when the ministry is carried out at some great distance from the congregation and without their direct involvement. A new vision of ministry to the world, one that also changes the faith lives of individual members by sending groups of members on mission trips, brings new energy and focus to the congregation and to members' faith. Embraced, the new vision changes the life cycle of the congregation to look more like the graph that follows:

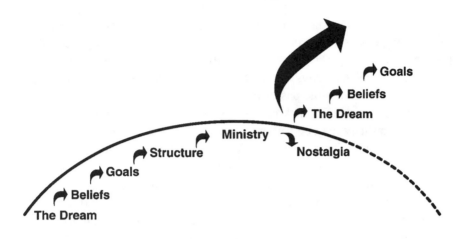

This is revisioning. When leaders interrupt nostalgia with this strategy, they find a healthy, energy- and life-providing form of change that allows both the members and the congregation to find new life. They reach out to respond to God's next call or challenge.

Restructuring looks very different. It too usually begins in the later stage of ministry or the stages of nostalgia and questioning. But rather than asking the discernment question, What are we called to next? it often asks the question, How do we fix and reenergize what we have? The cycle looks more like this:

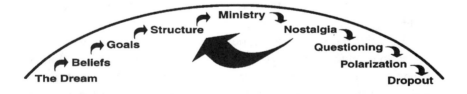

Restructuring is a return to the sections of the life cycle that many leaders and members in congregations like best—goals and structure. These are the steps and stages we remember fondly in our congregational histories because we remember how our work and our organized steps got us to the stage of ministry in the first place. We once again have the satisfaction of rolling up our sleeves and getting something done. We hope that if we do again what we did to achieve ministry in the earlier time, we will be able to repeat that ministry.

In a period of nostalgia or questioning, one of the first reactions is to set new goals or to restructure by changing one of three things: people, programs, or policy. As congregations slip into nostalgia and begin to miss the remembered days of the stage of ministry, they want to fix the situation by changing the pastor or other key leaders in the congregation. Or they want to set new policies or develop new programs. The dilemma is that they may be trying to return to a time of ministry that has already passed by. This is very much like the human life stages: It is inappropriate for older adults to try to recapture the full energy of youth, as well remembered as it may be. What is much more appropriate is for older adults to find new challenges and develop new skills and interests that fit with the new stage of life they are moving toward. The difference is between trying to recapture old history already gone and being open to new history not yet lived.

Restructuring in the congregation may be a very appropriate response. If the current practice of the stage of ministry is still appropriate to the congregation and its setting, restructuring may provide the support and the changes to keep the stage of ministry energized and vital. Setting new goals, developing new programs in the same target areas of ministry, changing leaders, may be very helpful and appropriate ways to reenergize a stage of ministry that is still valid. But if the issue is not revitalizing an appropriate ministry, if the issue is the need to dream again in order to vision a more faithful and effective future, restructuring is a collusive act. Inappropriately or unnecessarily changing people, programs, or policy may ultimately and intuitively be designed not to provide the very change the congregation seems to want.

For example, this pattern can be observed in many congregations that seek to change their clergy leadership because the congregation is no longer as active or vital as it once was. The congregation restructures by calling a new clergy leader. When communicating with their denominational leaders, they are very clear that they want a person who will be able to create change in the congregation. "We want someone who will help us reconnect with our community." Or, "We are looking for a pastor who will engage us spiritually and make worship an exciting event." Or, "We want someone who will interest our children in the faith and provide leadership in youth programming." The goal is to capture something that is now missing. The congregation restructures to achieve the new goal by providing a new leader.

And then as the new clergy leader arrives on the scene, members pull the new clergyperson aside, usually gently and graciously, and offer variations on the message, "Let me explain how we do things around here." In other words, the restructuring is designed collusively to *not* change the very thing that it was hoped to change. Such "solutions" are intuitively seen as solving our "problem" in ways that will not change "us." In other words, they guarantee that the congregation will not have to do anything differently or adjust to new people. Nonetheless, the congregation will have done *something*. And doing something is very satisfying for the immediate moment. The problem is that it does not work. Inappropriate restructuring is an effort to do again what we once did with the hope that it will make a difference. The level of change many congregations are facing, however, will not be addressed by these old answers and reworked efforts.

This is not a dilemma faced only by congregations. Governments, businesses, and institutions are all confronted with the same reality: Addressing new challenges with old answers does not work. In fact, many of our challenges are produced by overusing old assumptions, practices, and behaviors. For example, in an exploration of the workplace in a deeply changing society, Willis Harman of the Institute of Noetic Sciences offers compelling examples of this dilemma related to our use of technology.

> A measure of our confusion is that we continue to try to solve the problems that have been brought about or exacerbated by our use of technology with more technology used in the same way! The most egregious example is creating Star Wars to combat the threat of nuclear missiles, but there are others: attempting to cure ecological insults brought about by our use of technology through a "pollution control industry"; dealing with illness caused in part by modern lifestyles through interventions such as chemotherapy and radiation that further impair the natural healing and defense systems; seeking technological cures for chronic poverty and hunger that are themselves the consequences of industrial society impinging on other cultures.[2]

One of the sayings of organizational change and quality management that continues to surface in business and corporations is the definition of "insanity": doing the same thing over and over and expecting different results. It is a testament to the experience that trying to solve a problem using the same tools (assumptions, ideas, behaviors) that got us into the problem does not work. This is true whether we are looking at a problem situation or at a situation where a new dream or vision is seeking to break through. We often cannot take the next step in an environment of great change if we insist on using old tools and methodologies.

A Game

Idea: There is a saying that Frederick the Great (1712-1786) lost the battle of Jena (1806). This means that for twenty years after his death, the army perpetuated his form of organization instead of adapting to meet changes in the art of war.

Group Discussion: What seven ideas and practices in your congregation that have been successful in the past are limiting your congregational growth, your congregational leadership, or your programs? Who would be surprised to hear what you describe? Why would they be surprised?

Leaders need to risk moving beyond the collusive act of spinning wheels in ways guaranteed not to change our congregations. They need to risk seeking new ways to look at the future. But they also need to risk speaking the truth and acknowledging that the old ways and old assumptions are collusive. The old ways may feel comfortable and safe. They permit us to be satisfyingly active. But they allow us to avoid change.

Leaders can move past the collusive nonchange of restructuring by doing the up-front homework that will allow them to know the right way to talk to the congregation, and the right issue or topic to talk to the congregation about—one that will open the door to change.

Force Field Analysis

There is a rather old but highly effective strategy to identify the key collusive issues that can keep a congregation from moving ahead into necessary change. "Force field analysis" is a tool to help leaders identify
and describe "driving" and "resisting" forces operative in the congregation as a way to strategize next steps. It is based on the assumption that a
system held in equilibrium (nonchange) is held there by the opposing but
balanced driving (⇨) and resisting (⇦) forces.

Force field analysis began with the work of Kurt Lewin, a German
psychologist who emigrated to the United States in 1933 to teach at
Cornell University.[3] Lewin was an originator of action research, which
is at the foundation of much of the understanding of organizations and
groups today. He was also one of the earliest proponents of the "learning
organization," which stresses the importance of involving people in
learning about their own situation and helping to determine the decisions
and steps to be taken in response. A core principle of change Lewin introduced stated that "we are likely to modify our own behavior when we
participate in problem analysis and solution and likely to carry out decisions we have helped make."[4] In fact, he conceived of a novel form of
problem solving that could be called "doing by learning."[5] Force field
analysis is a clear example of this: Groups of leaders are invited to describe in detail the forces influencing their situation and then choose
steps to shift the balance toward a wanted change.

Force field analysis may best be understood using a frequently told
story about Lewin that might be apocryphal. According to the story, during World War II the United States military turned to Kurt Lewin for
help because of his reputation for understanding groups and organizational dynamics. The problem was that the soldiers in the war effort were
not willing to eat liver when it was served. A backlog of crates of liver
was creating a storage and financial problem for the military administra-
tors and a morale problem for the cooks in the kitchens.

Lewin is said to have explained to the military leaders that their
problem was an example of equilibrium: The forces to make soldiers eat
the liver were balanced by the forces of resistance from the soldiers who
did not want to eat the liver. To solve the problem, Lewin suggested the
military leaders begin by describing the driving forces used to get the
soldiers to eat liver and the resisting forces that made the soldiers not

want to eat the liver. The list produced looked something like the following:

Driving Forces	Resisting Forces
It is the food being served. If you don't eat it nothing else is available. ⇨	⇦ Many people think it tastes bad.
	⇦ The texture is unappealing.
There is an oversupply of it. ⇨	⇦ It smells bad.
It is a very healthy food and good for you. ⇨	⇦ Soldiers want some control over what they eat.
The Army has told you to eat it. ⇨	
It is an inexpensive meat. ⇨	

There are two very helpful insights that can be gained by doing a force field analysis. The first is that by simply describing all of the forces involved in moving toward or resisting a change, one has a much clearer idea of what issues or ideas need to be addressed. They are not always the most obvious ones. The second helpful insight is the principle that Lewin is said to have explained to the military leaders: Change is managed better *when you address and decrease the resisters* than when you simply increase the drivers and try to force the change.

If the military simply reinforced the drivers and told soldiers that they must eat the liver because there was an oversupply, because it was an inexpensive meal, because it was good for them, or any other persuasive arguments, the predictable result would be increased resistance. In order to maintain systemic balance, the natural response of the soldiers would be to increase their complaints about the liver. Instead of trying to persuade or force the soldiers to eat liver, Lewin suggested that the cooks reduce the resisting forces by preparing the liver smothered in onions and bacon. By doing so they would be reducing the perceptions of unappealing texture, unpleasant smell, and unappetizing taste. The natural balance of the situation would then rather easily tilt toward the change the army was seeking. And the result would be that soldiers would more willingly eat the liver. The story as usually told ends with the soldiers being willing to eat the liver and the military returning its attention to the war.

Whether the story is true or not, it is regularly repeated at academic gatherings that focus on Lewin's work because the principles are accurate. When leaders are able to identify the significant issues that create the balance between drive and resistance, and when they are able to reduce the resistance *and* support the drivers toward change, the balance rather naturally moves in the direction the leaders are seeking. In other words, weakening resisters is a more effective strategy for change than is trying to convince followers about the truth of the drivers.

Example: Establishing a Shelter

Let's look at a small group of mid-size urban congregations that were trying to lead their members and their community to provide emergency shelter for men during winter months. All of the congregations involved were part of an urban coalition that had for years addressed human need. The history of this coalition was rich with examples of members actively and aggressively reaching out to help others in need. They had developed programs providing food and clothing, supported a community medical clinic, carried out an active outreach of visitation to the elderly, and advocated with the city government and local hospitals for people who did not speak English as their first language. And yet, after three years of preparatory work they had still not been able to open an emergency shelter for men. The leaders' frustration was increased by the fact that during those same years, several emergency shelters had been made available to women and children. Finally the leaders of the coalition spent a full afternoon developing a force field analysis of their experience. The drivers and the resisters included the following:

Driving Forces		Resisting Forces
We can identify the men who need the shelter. ⇨	⇦	It is difficult to get insurance coverage for the church providing shelter.
Women and children have emergency shelter. ⇨	⇦	People are concerned over the upkeep and care of the chosen facility.
We have available facitlities ⇨ and volunteers.		
Providing such care is the ⇨ stated mission of our coalition and our congregations.	⇦	According to the Protestant work ethic, men should take care of themselves.
	⇦	People are afraid of community reaction.
Such programs are a part ⇨ of our history.		

The leaders recognized that if they continued to stress driving forces on the left side of the analysis, the increased drivers (persuasion) would produce increased resistance from the members of their own congregations. For example, sharing more information about the numbers of homeless men would fall on deaf and resistant ears. Instead, they set about understanding the resisters on the right side of the analysis. After discussion they realized issues of insurance and facility concerns were problems that had solutions and that these were not the critical resisters. And they recognized that negative community reaction was not going to diminish, no matter what they did. In fact, they recalled that their history of community ministry was filled with examples of negative community reaction. But community reaction had never stopped them before.

It was then that they began to realize the importance of the resistance related to the Protestant work ethic. People believed that if a man was without shelter, it was both his fault and his problem to solve. The same ethic did not apply to women and children. The community was much more willing to see them as appropriately dependent on others for help, and the consequence was that shelters were available for women and children in this community. But the community clearly held a different standard for men.

It became clear to the leaders that they would have to address and weaken this resister force if emergency shelter for men was ever to become a possibility in that community. The members of their congregations and of the community were going to have to *learn* something new before they would be able to *do* something new.

From these insights an appropriate strategy began to develop. The leaders of the coalition knew homeless men through the congregations' food and clothing programs (a driver from the left side of the analysis). They began to interview these men, inviting them to tell their personal stories about how they ended up being homeless. The leaders used these personal stories to educate their congregations. They uncovered a number of stories of alcoholism and talked to their congregations about alcoholism as a disease instead of a choice. There were also a number of men who were homeless who had recently been cared for in a local mental hospital. But as legislation changed the rules about who could remain under hospital care and for how long, these men had been released into the community and had not been able to care for themselves. The leaders began to teach their congregations about the effect of deinstitutionalization.

The most persuasive single story that they uncovered, however, was about a man who had been sleeping under a local bridge for several months but who held a full-time job and who reported to work every day. This man had been living with his wife and their child in a small apartment in the city. But he and his wife were having problems with their marriage, and they were going to separate. With only enough money available for one apartment, this man voluntarily gave the apartment to his family and lived without shelter himself.

When the personal stories of a number of these homeless men (without their names attached, of course) were shared with members of the congregations, the resistance to emergency shelter decreased dramatically. Steps to begin a trial shelter for the winter months on a limited basis were supported, and a pilot emergency shelter was opened within six months.

The leaders of the coalition broke the collusive cycle of leading by doing and used the force field analysis to identify what needed to be learned, not done. In times of great change a critical responsibility of leaders is to identify and to respond to what needs to be learned. Often this means identifying what the leaders themselves must learn.

Example: Finding "Good" Members

I was working with a program board of a congregation, and in the course of the work board members began to criticize and complain about not receiving new members. I was puzzled by the conversation, because I had seen the statistics that clearly indicated that new members regularly joined this congregation at a rate that kept it growing modestly. That meant that each year the congregation received enough new members to replace the ones who moved out of this very transient area plus a few more members who would support gradual growth.

When I asked about their complaining and pointed to the numbers of new members they were receiving, they responded, "Oh, but those are not *good* members." Shocked at the response, I invited the people at the meeting to describe a "good" member. What we learned was that for this group of forty- to sixty-five-year-old congregational leaders, a good member was one who attended worship regularly, participated in adult education classes, volunteered to be on at least one committee, showed up at most social functions at the congregation, participated in special programs or projects, and supported the budget through regular giving. To no one's surprise, not even theirs, they had described themselves.

We then quickly described what the last one hundred new members of that congregation would look like if they all stood together in the same room at the same time. What these program leaders described was a group of people mostly between the ages of twenty-one to thirty-five with several young children. In most cases both parents were employed full-time or only one parent lived with the children. It quickly became clear that these new members were not "good" members (according to the program board members' criteria), because the lifestyle of the new members would not allow such a high level of activity and involvement in the worship and programs of the congregation.

The program board members needed to learn. They needed to learn about the lifestyle and demands faced by younger, dual-income families. They needed to learn about sharing "their" pool of volunteers with other community groups and agencies. They needed to learn how to plan congregational programs that were not heavily committee-dependent and labor intensive for people who did not have time and interest in being on committees. Without such learnings, this program board would have remained in the "doing" mode and continued to plan and offer programs that many of the new members were too busy and overloaded to attend. And the collusive division between old and new members would have continued in such a way that the feelings between the two groups increasingly deteriorated but the life of the congregation went unchanged. Clearly providing leadership in a time of change does not always require leaders to do something and come up with the right answer. In fact, this may exacerbate the problem, or even worse, collusively sidestep it. Rather than do, leaders are at times called to learn—and to teach others what they are learning.

Asking the Right Questions

Change in the congregation can also be aided by using the appropriate strategy or approach when asking people to respond to change. What escapes many leaders is that there are different ways to introduce and invite a response to change. Congregations do not always need to follow learned behavior and make decisions or initiate change "the way we've always done it." This syndrome hides other alternatives that may be more helpful and healthy.

It is easy to see this as we move from one group to another. For example, I often work with governing boards that make decisions by simple majority votes. In this case every board member has one vote that is equal to the one vote every other board member holds. Although this is standard decision-making practice for many boards, I do not assume this is the only way groups make decisions. I do not assume, for example that all decisions in a family would be made using the one-person-one-vote principle. When my sons were in elementary or secondary school, their votes did not equal mine or my wife's in family decisions. We used other methods to seek agreement for decisions.

By demonstrating that the way we seek decisions and agreement for change can shift from group to group, leaders are helped to understand that methods or strategies also can change from situation to situation. Yet it is not uncommon for leaders to get stuck when trying to get agreement because they are using a strategy that is not helpful.

Calvin Pava of the Harvard Business School demonstrates that the way leaders ask for change can be approached strategically by looking at the complexity of the situation and the level of conflict involved in the change being faced.[6] By complexity Pava means the "messiness" of the situation and the number of intertwined or unstable conditions that exist. (Are there a lot of factors that need to be considered, and are they difficult to distinguish clearly from one another?) By conflict he refers to the level (low to high) of interdependence and divergence people feel with each other around the issue being considered.[7] (To what extent do people need to depend on one another in the situation, and do they have different assumptions or needs related to the outcome?) Although these two variables—complexity and conflict—may be intuitive measures that leaders need to guess at, they do suggest alternative approaches or strategies for change.

Following are four strategies adapted from Pava's categories of complexity and conflict.[8] They raise again the issue of "appropriateness." Are leaders asking for decisions or seeking change in the congregation in the most helpful ways?

Low Task Complexity   High Task Complexity

	Low Conflict	High Conflict

Low Conflict

Straightforward Linear Planning

- define the problem and the preferred solution
- move to action plans

Normative Systems Redesign

- reformulate the problem
- involve widespread participation
- seek ownership of the process
- redesign of system

High Conflict

Incremental Nonplanning

- bargain
- negotiate
- vote
- adjudicate

Disorderly ("nonsynoptic") Planning
(an indirect approach to system wide change)

- use unclear objectives
- use imprecise methods
- encourage disorderly action
- use tacit emphasis on changing the system

Passive Response ⟵   ⟶ **Active Response**

An exploration of the four quadrants of Pava's model suggests practical guidelines for choosing an appropriate change strategy. *Quadrant I* is a situation of low conflict and low complexity that requires *straightforward linear planning* as an appropriate strategy. A typical example in many congregations may be the decision about how a bequest of money is to be used. Although this may be a sensitive decision, it is often low complexity and low conflict. It is appropriately approached with the classic problem-solving method that most of us know best and use most frequently:

Problem ➪ How will we use this additional financial resource?
Brainstorm ➪ What are the available options?
Decision ➪ What is the best choice from our available options?

Similarly, seeking to include more laity in leading worship is a quadrant I example in many congregations. The task or question is relatively clear and people are not highly divided on the outcome. Such a straightforward planning strategy is helpful in giving people the information they need to make an informed choice.

Quadrant II is a situation with a similarly clear task, but people are more dependent on one another and there is some conflict about the different expectations people hold about the outcome. This situation requires *incremental nonplanning,* because decisions need to be made but will not be accomplished with full and easy agreement. There will be "winners" and "losers" with the outcome. As Pava notes, "Intense differences give rise to suspicion and malice that impede major change efforts. Yet low complexity makes it possible to obtain acceptable outcomes with marginal alterations and partial solutions."[9]

Recently I was working with a congregation through a rather complex set of negotiations about their future. Members had very different understandings and expectations. In the midst of this we came to the point of electing a new person to a key leadership position for the next year. The person nominated was highly controversial because of positions he had taken relative to the negotiations we were involved with. The task of election, however, was simple and straightforward. Board members indicated very quickly that they understood the implications of this election and the need to move ahead with a decision. We made sure everyone understood that election would be by simple majority.

We agreed to use written ballots. The election was held, the nominated person was elected, and the board returned to the more complex problems at hand. This was clearly an example of quadrant II "incremental nonplanning." A clear, straightforward decision was made in which there were intense differences among board members. But the low complexity of the task and its implications allowed the board to address it directly, accept the results, and move on.

Quadrant III is a situation of high task complexity but low conflict. *Normative systems redesign* is the appropriate approach when many variables need to be considered and many new learnings need to be discovered. Simple problem solving and straightforward negotiating or voting are not helpful strategies in this situation. When describing this strategy Pava notes:

> Low conflict and high uncertainty foster conditions that require a more comprehensive change strategy. Task uncertainty manifests itself in the form of imprecise problems; the nature of difficulties is poorly defined and changes rapidly. Before change can begin, this mess must be parsed into a workable problem. The absence of high conflict means that different interests can work jointly to formulate a problem and rectify it.[10]

In this strategy the issues facing the congregation are broken down and identified using categories such as worship, programs, facilities, finances, leadership, and so forth. An effort is made to involve and to listen to the needs and interests of a large portion of the congregation in small-group meetings or house meetings. Leaders are careful to communicate back to the members what they have heard and how the information received from members has been used to help shape decisions or next steps. This is done so that members can clearly see that their voices have been taken into account and so that they can "own" the results. And then the congregation's worship, or programs, or finances, are redesigned according to these new learnings.

Normative systems redesign is a fairly common planning strategy for many congregations. It requires a good deal of coordination and oversight by the central leaders or planners to keep all of the component parts of the complex situation related to the bigger picture facing the congregation. But in a complex setting with low congregational conflict, this strategy of change is highly effective.

A less known change strategy is described in Pava's *Quadrant IV* disorderly or *nonsynoptic systems change* model.

> Simultaneously high levels of complexity and conflict favor a novel approach: nonsynoptic systems change. Nonsynoptic systems change methods appears fragmented or disorderly ("nonsynoptic"), yet their aim is to trigger some kind of thorough-going alteration (system-wide change). This approach seems contradictory, blending comprehensiveness and incrementalism. But the mix of high complexity and high conflict make this concoction essential. High complexity requires systemwide change, encompassing a variety of factors. Simultaneously, a high level of conflict makes an indirect approach necessary, to avoid polarizing groups that already diverge. This requires an indirect approach to systemic change, with unclear objectives, imprecise methods, disorderly action, and tacit emphasis on changing an entire system.[11]

In its description the quadrant IV strategy no doubt sounds as confusing and messy as the situation it is proposed to respond to. It acknowledges, however, that there are some situations or change environments that are complex and tense enough that they will not respond well to structured control. Rather than trying to control and direct the change, in quadrant IV leaders seek to remove barriers and open up opportunities supportive of change. What directs the change is a general description of the hoped-for results and an invitation for the various parties in the congregation to work to get there.

An example that may be familiar to many congregational leaders can be found in a typical strategy used by middle judicatory leaders. Middle judicatory programs and events are often the focal point of highly diverse interests. Decisions and policies are influenced by participants' gender, race, age, theological, political, and financial differences. Agreement is difficult to achieve because of the complexity and the differences in expectations that face leaders. Efforts to achieve agreement and change using linear planning models and normative systems redesign create battlegrounds where conflicting forces engage each other. Resorting to an incremental nonplanning model (voting, negotiating, and adjudication) may be of help in specific instances, but on a larger scale this model brings the region, conference, or synod to a grinding halt as intense energy is put into negotiating in a way that will produce winners and losers. In such a situation, change is more appropriately addressed by announcing the theme or the direction of the change rather than trying to control and direct it. Once the direction is announced, the various parties and groups that belong to the middle judicatory are invited to work within their own area of responsibility to make the theme come alive. The invitation is not to coordinate their efforts with all other groups. Nor does this strategy require agreement over the strategy or steps participants will use to address the theme. Instead each party is to use its own gifts and strengths to help bring life to the overall effort within the context of its own responsibilities. Such "themes" are typically announced or set at the annual middle judicatory or denominational meeting. General themes may take the form of statements such as "Making God's Love and Justice Known" or "Calling Local Congregations to Transformation" or "Calling People to New Life in Jesus Christ."

Rather than hammering out a specific plan in which each party understands and agrees on how the theme is to be implemented, each group is invited to incorporate the theme into its year's work and to strategize ways to implement the theme. Efforts at coordination are minimal, which gives some sense of why Pava calls this disorderly or nonsynoptic planning. But the lack of coordination and control minimizes disruptive conflict, because the parties are not required to seek agreement and common territory. The larger system then begins to change as individual parts begin to focus on the theme. Evaluation and accountability are managed, again, not by questioning coordinated efforts but by descriptive questions, such as, "What have you done this past year to make God's love and justice known?" or "… to call congregations to transformation?"

An example in a smaller setting can be found in the "systems-centered training" of Yvonne Agazarian, a therapist widely known for her work as a group-as-a-whole theoretician. In an effort to manage rather than control the way her training groups related to their own organization, Agazarian introduced "functional management." Using the organization's newsletter, she invited all members to make the goals of the systems-centered training program achievable through their own initiative. She did not seek to direct the developments and changes, although the leaders would manage the changes initiated by the members. The invitation in the newsletter stated:

Functional Management, as we are conceptualizing it, is managing by the act of functioning in management roles related to SCT (systems-centered training) goals....

How we make functional management happen is to make the newsletter the major communication link between SCT members and SCT management. *Who* will have input will be every SCT member who reads their newsletter and wants to take their own authority.[12]

Although this method may feel messy and imprecise, it encourages and empowers change at a much greater pace than would be possible if agreement were necessary at each step along the way. Congregations intuitively use quadrant IV methods when individuals or subgroups within the congregation have special concerns or gifts that they do not want to deny but cannot align with the full life of the congregation. For example, a small group that has committed itself to simple living may be invited to add its concern and commitment for a specific lifestyle to the educational and missional program of the congregation without seeking agreement that the whole congregation commit itself to simple living.

What is less common, but potentially productive, is for congregations to set major directions for change and then invite individuals and groups within the congregation to initiate their own efforts to achieve the goals without first seeking agreement and common steps for all to follow. This strategy will support change without engaging conflict over the differences that exist in the congregation. And rather than controlling and directing the change, leaders manage and support the change as it occurs. Rather than having to resolve all differences, leaders can respond to competing efforts in the congregation and invite members to learn by explaining to each other why they have such different approaches to the same goal.

Exercises for Leaders

The following diagnostic conversations are meant to invite an intuitive awareness of where your congregation may be in the process of change and what is needed from leaders. Leaders are invited to use their own experience and information to test whether there is agreement on what the congregation is facing.

1. Using the model of the life cycle of the congregation, invite leaders to discuss the following questions:

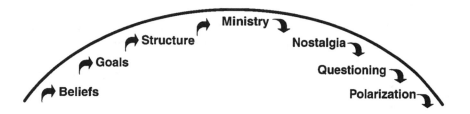

A. At what stage of the life cycle is the critical mass of our congregation? What evidence can you offer to support your description?

B. Is it appropriate for us to restructure or revision?

- Are we trying to recapture a time and a form of ministry that has passed us by and can no longer be faithful for our future? (inappropriate restructuring)
- Are we trying to reenergize a form of ministry that is still appropriate for our call by God and that still attracts and engages members spiritually? (appropriate restructuring)
- Do we need to break out of old forms of ministry and ask what is required of us next in order to be faithful and engage people in our ministry? (appropriate revisioning)

2. Do a force field analysis for a situation of change your board or congregation is facing:

A. Describe the goal of your change: "The goal is to ..."

B. List all the driving and resisting forces you can identify:

Drivers	Resisters

C. Strategize how to weaken or respond to the key resisting forces as a way of supporting the persuasive nature of the driving forces.

3. Identify an issue or a decision for change facing your board or congregation. Using Pava's four-quadrant strategy model, discuss the following questions:

A. How complex is this issue or decision? Are a number of variables connected to it, or is it fairly clear and straightforward?

B. What level of conflict is related to this issue or decision? Do people hold a number of diverse interests? Have people stated clear positions about this issue or decision that are in opposition to positions held by other people?

C. Based on your responses to questions A and B, which change strategies seem appropriate for your congregation? How would you implement an appropriate strategy to deal with the issue or decision?

CHAPTER 7

A Postscript for the Faith Community: Behavior Appropriate to a Congregation

A fanatic is one who can't change his mind and won't change the subject.

—attributed to Sir Winston Churchill

The following excerpt is from a report written to a congregation experiencing problems in a time of transition. The full report was sixteen pages long and summarized the steps I took to learn about their situation, a description of the issues they faced, and recommendations for next steps they could take to address their situation. The name of the congregation has been changed for two reasons. The first, obviously, is to protect the congregation. The second reason is to suggest that this portion of the report increasingly belongs to a growing number of congregations wrestling with difficult or inappropriate behavior among staff, leaders, and members as they face problems and situations of change.

"Before leaving this descriptive statement of the larger context in which Old First Church finds itself, there are two other issues that have played a role in the current experience. The first is the "culture" of Old First Church. There are certain characteristics of this congregation that exacerbate the discomfort among its members. Characteristics that give Old First Church its unique identity and personality include:

- *its critical nature. One member called the church "hypercritical" and another stated, "People complain about absolutely everything here." In general, when church members attend "listening groups" and fill out questionnaires, as was done at*

*Old First Church, it is common for the composite list of responses
to include nearly equal numbers of strengths and weaknesses. It is
not unusual, even with churches experiencing deep conflict, to list
more strengths than weaknesses. As a very rough measure of the
"critical culture" at Old First Church, it needs to be noted that
the list of weaknesses is more than double the length of identified
strengths.*

*• its style of indirect communication. Concerns and criticisms
are routinely shared in side conversations with others long before
they are addressed directly with the persons involved or the committee responsible. Rumors and unsubstantiated stories are ap-
parently passed freely among persons. It was a very frequent experience of the consultant to hear one explanation of an event or
a relationship between two persons and then to hear the direct opposite explanation of the same event or relationship from others.
The listening groups consistently provided examples of people
who prefaced their statements by saying: "I heard ...," indicating
that they were not speaking from personal experience. In many
cases the validity of a story or a criticism was based on a member's
respect for the person who was their source of the information,
rather than any substantiation of fact."*

*This section of the report was not initially received well by a num-
ber of people in the congregation. Although congregations often are
sensitive and initially defensive when someone holds up and describes
inappropriate or unhelpful behavior, the more thoughtful response
that eventually develops is to recognize and admit that manageable
problems have become unmanageable because of inappropriate behavior. Once appropriate behaviors are practiced, leaders find it
much easier to address difficult situations.*

Change increases anxiety. People who feel pushed into change respond with active resistance as they seek to restore an equilibrium that
seems threatened. The give and take, the push and pull, is not always
gracious. Surprised people tend to behave badly.

The above descriptions are not unique to faith communities. The
tug-of-war and battle for control also go on culturally, and we increas-

ingly hear people decry the current lack of civility. We observe poor behavior in our government, work places, school boards and civic associations, families ... and congregations. Part of the apparent cost of change
in the congregation is the disappointment of witnessing insensitive and
impatient behavior. We struggle with people (including ourselves) who
are driven to "win," and we experience withdrawal and brokenness in
relationships with people who leave because they "certainly don't expect that kind of behavior in the congregation."

Civility does seem to be getting squeezed in our time. We are increasingly recognized as the most litigious society on the globe, turning
to lawsuits to right perceived wrongs even before we consider actual
conversation between the aggrieved parties to see whether something
can be done to resolve the issue. The lack of consideration and respect
has been stretched and worn between Republican and Democratic fed-
eral legislators, so much so that a "relationship building retreat" was
held for senators and representatives at the end of 1996 to try to rebuild
civility in their working relationships. School boards and home-owner
associations in planned communities are increasingly forced to make decisions in response to confrontation and pressure groups rather than
through proactive strategies to address planning and development. This
broad cultural pattern is also influencing the way congregational leaders
and members address and engage one another during times of change,
when anxiety has risen.

A Matter of Manners

Philosopher and former university president John Silber was both accurate and helpful when he identified this demise of civility as a lack of
manners. But he was clear to point out that manners are about more than
simple polite behavior. Quoting John Fletcher Moulton, Silber identified three domains of human interaction.

> Seventy-five years ago ... Lord Moulton, a noted English judge,
> spoke on the subject of "Law and Manners." He divided human ac-
> tion into three domains. The first is the domain of law, "where," he
> said, "our actions are prescribed by laws binding upon us which
> must be obeyed." At the other extreme is the domain of free choice,

"which," he said, "includes all those actions as to which we claim and enjoy complete freedom." And in between, Lord Moulton identified a domain in which our action is not determined by law but in which we are not free to behave in any way we choose....

Lord Moulton considered the area of action lying between law and pure personal preference to be "the domain of obedience to the unenforceable." In this domain, he said, "obedience is the obedience of a man to that which he cannot be forced to obey. He is the enforcer of the law upon himself." This domain between law and free choice he called that of manners. While it may include moral duty, social responsibility, and proper behavior, it extends beyond them to cover "all cases of doing right where there is no one to make you do it but yourself."[1]

Today we attend little to the domain of manners, "obedience to the unenforceable." Much attention is given to legislative answers, efforts to enforce agreement and conformity (for example, in areas as critical as abortion, prayer, and welfare). Advocates of such legislation seek to extend the domain of law. They seek to legislate right behavior. We have also inherited the spirit of immediate gratification from the movements of the 1960s, and the indomitable spirit of the individual from American frontiers. This heritage lies in the domain of free choice. As we struggle to live in these two areas, the helpful and healthy behaviors in the domain of manners have been diminished. A simple graphic of this experience might look something like the following.

THE DOMAIN ⇨ MANNERS AND OBEDIENCE ⇦ THE DOMAIN OF
OF LAW   TO THE UNENFORCEABLE   FREE CHOICE

In a faith community, "manners" does not refer only to socially appropriate behavior. Manners in congregations also reflect the teachings and values of faith. These teachings and values are a part of the unenforceable domain because they are not laws, and we are not free to disregard them. Unlike laws or rigid rules that once broken will result in punishment, the manners of faith are to be found in covenants or promises to practice behaviors grounded in the teachings in the congregation. Loving others because we have first been loved by God is not a law. But neither do people in congregations have the free choice to behave unlovingly toward others. Seeking ways to be loving and caring to others is grounded in the manners of faith—obedience to the unenforceable. We are not required by law or denominational rules to forgive repeatedly (seventy times seven). But neither are we free not to forgive others.

This too is grounded in the manners of faith. Congregations as faith communities need to be able to depend on the practice of obedience to the unenforceable as a context for the shared practice of the faith. We do not have faith or practice the disciplines of our faith *alone*. And the values and behaviors of the faith community often stand in contrast to and, at times, against the values and behaviors of the culture. Claiming to be different from our culture, we should not accept insensitive, uncaring, or irresponsible behavior in our congregations—even during anxious times of change when differences are most pronounced. My very good friend and exceptionally able preacher Fred Day made this point in a sermon about the widow who brought her tithe to the Temple. Jesus referred to the widow's sacrificial giving saying, "She gave from her want all she had to live on" (Mark 12:44). Fred then asked in his sermon:

> How about the widow in the Gospel? Would you hold her up as an example to your children? Our most likely reaction, probably, is that the widow's action is an ideal, not a norm for daily conduct. When there is a conflict between the values presented us, the society in which we live and the values presented in the Gospel, we usually question the Gospel values first.[2]

How do we help our congregations hold fast to their faith values and question instead the values of the culture? Fred also included a story about a young child who was treated by a psychotherapist because of his literal application of lessons he had learned in Sunday school. Following treatment the child was reported to be "cured of his Christian preoccupation" and therefore "normal." I suggest that leaders of congregations not allow the culture to "cure" members of a preoccupation with faith values. We do not need to give in to win/lose strategies that we mistakenly think of as "the democratic way." Instead, I invite leaders to risk claiming and practicing faith values during times of change. This practice of faith values might begin at a level as fundamental as doing unto others as we would have them do unto us as we wrestle with the issues facing our congregation.

Providing a Safe Environment

Although leaders might not be able to provide a solution or a direction
that will satisfy all the parties concerned, they can provide, and are responsible for providing, a safe environment in which people can search
for solutions and directions. We cannot assume that such a safe environment already exists in our congregations. Faith communities tend not to
be well practiced in dealing with differences. The history of many congregations and denominations suggests that differences and diversity
lead to schism and broken community, rather than to a more faithful future. In his brief book on living with diversity, pastor and author Stephen
Kliewer is correct in noting that "a church cannot just sit back and hope
that [a safe environment] will develop naturally. The church leadership
must consciously take the lead in the shaping of the atmosphere, developing a dynamic that will support the presence of diverse elements within the church."[3]

It should be noted that leaders' efforts to provide a safe environment should be initiated sooner rather than later when congregations are
facing change. In fact, although it is never too late, it is much healthier
for leaders to agree on appropriate and respectful behaviors before they
need to make decisions about matters that will bring out differences. It
is much more difficult to stop in the midst of a confrontation to talk
about the way people will behave with one another. For example, if
prior to exploring a controversial issue at a board meeting all board
members are asked to agree not to speak a second time until everyone
has had opportunity to offer a first statement, the request may be perceived as a tool that ensures healthy and inclusive conversation. If the
same agreement is suggested midway through a tense meeting, however,
those who have been speaking often may think this is a measure to control them, and those who have been silent may perceive the new rule as
a strategy to get them to take sides. When the prospect of change is on
the horizon, it is healthier for leaders to begin exploring agreements and
behaviors before engaging the issues in order to help participants deal
with their differences. With behavioral and attitudinal agreements in
hand, different opinions and needs related to change will be more easily
managed with maturity and respect.

Congregations are often ill prepared to deal with the anxiety and
differences produced by change because members assume that "our faith

holds us together" and "we are above all that." One of the lessons of the computer age is that there are certain "default" settings in life. Unless you intentionally change the setting, the computer will "default" to margins, font, and other settings already set. Similarly, unless leaders intentionally change the agreements and the environment in which they will explore and decide on issues of change, they will "default" to cultural strategies: confrontation, a win/lose agenda, and less than civil behavior. Congregational leaders and members alike are often embarrassed to observe the default behavior. The behavior also carries a spiritual cost for people who find themselves witnessing or participating in behaviors that do not fit the values and behaviors proclaimed by the standards of their faith.

The Value of Conflict

One of the first steps leaders can take to develop a safe environment in the midst of change is to recognize and honor the value that conflict holds for them. In the idealized congregation, there is no conflict. But in the healthy congregation, there is. One of the realities leaders need to accept is that without healthy conflict in their congregation—without conflict in their board meetings, in the relationships between clergy and laity, between staff and volunteers, between long-term and short-term members—there is no life or energy. But what leaders also need to accept is that *conflict is not the same thing as a fight!*

Somewhere along the way in my training and my work with congregations, I picked up this operational definition of conflict: "Conflict is two or more ideas in the same place at the same time." I continue to remind myself and the congregations that I work with about that definition. It helps me and others to see that if we do not have two or more ideas to work with, then we are without life, without direction, without energy. If a congregation has lived with only one idea for an extended time, then it is committed to the status quo, to what already is. And it is fairly easy for people to be able to see that a long-term commitment to the status quo in an environment of great change is an untenable position with very little prospect for either faithfulness or survival.

Still, the lessons of healthy and productive conflict come hard for many congregations and leaders. They point to their assumptions about the power of their shared faith and the way people will behave and the need for harmony. Such assumptions need to be examined. For example, members often talk about the importance of harmony in the congregation. The same members, however, do not often consider that harmony does not come without differences. "????Harmony????" writes author Wally Armbruster. "If everybody's singing the same note that ain't harmony. That, baby, is monotony. Harmony happens when people sing different notes ... and even some which sound (at first) like discord suddenly start to sound great ... once your ear gets used to the idea."[4] Helping leaders understand the real differences between ideas such as conflict and fight, harmony and monotony, can offer rich insights into their purpose and performance as leaders.

It does not matter where you dip into the faith story—the pronouncements of Jeremiah and Ezekiel, the wrestling with God in the Psalms, the arguments over who will lead the community of 1 Corinthians, Jesus' challenges to his disciples and bystanders alike, the arguments between Paul and Peter—there is plenty of conflict through which congregations can view and understand their own differences. Biblical study is a means of helping congregations become more realistic about the wrestling they need to do. And it can help leaders to see that this wrestling is a fundamental faith task of the local congregation. When looking at congregations as "bearers of the tradition," that is, as the institutions that pass faith onto the next generation, it is helpful to understand that the congregation is most alive and the tradition most effectively passed on when its "members are engaged in a vibrant, embodied argument."[5] When addressing change and dealing with differences, leaders would do well to understand the importance of "holy argument," which is much more a part of our heritage and health than is false and empty harmony.

There is, however, a great difference between conflict and a fight, between learning and winning. Conflict can be either healthy and productive or unhealthy and destructive. For example, in a study of the difference between casualties and productive results of encounter group experiences, researchers M. A. Lieberman, I. D. Yalom, and M. B. Miles indicate that the critical factor determining whether conflict will make contributions is not whether it is present or absent. It is rather the management or mismanagement of the conflict that inherently exists which makes the difference.[6] Consider how a group of congregational leaders could be helped by being aware of the differences between healthy and unhealthy conflict as outlined below.[7]

Healthy	**Unhealthy**
1 ATTITUDE: Conflict is inevitable; it is a chance to grow.	ATTITUDE: Conflict is wrong or sinful.
2 PERSONALIZED: Disputants are clearly able to see the difference between the people and the problems and do not mix the two.	PERSONALIZED: Disputants quickly mix people and problems together and assume by changing or eliminating the people that the problem will be solved.
3 COMMUNICATION is open, people speak directly to one another and everyone has the same information	COMMUNICATION is diminished with people only speaking to those with whom they already agree. Third parties or letters are used to carry messages.
4 THE BALANCE SHEET is short. The principals address the issue at hand, not what happened months or years ago.	THE BALANCE SHEET is long. The list of grievances grows and examples are collected. People recall not only what they think was done to them, but what was said or done to their friends as well.
5 THE CHURCH IS INTERACTIVE. There is give and take and exchange of ideas and a spirit of cooperation and openness. There is careful listening and thought-out statements.	THE CHURCH IS REACTIVE. It cannot be "touched" without exploding. I write a memo to you and you immediately fire back a nasty letter to me.
6 ACCEPTANCE: Disputants acknowledge the existence of a problem and the need to solve it.	DENIAL: Disputants tend to ignore the real problems and deny what is going on.
7 TIMELINESS: Resolution takes as much time as needed. The parties involved take the time to go through the journey together, to experience the pain, and to come out together on the other side.	LACK OF TIME: There is a strong need to solve the problems too quickly. People are very "solution-oriented" and seek to avoid the pain of conflict by saying: "Let's get it over with."

Awareness of these differences and discussion of these assumptions, practices, and behaviors can support the work leaders must do in change. Using training resources about conflict during board meetings or retreats is an effective strategy and opportunity to help leaders prepare themselves. Several suggested resources are listed in the endnotes.[8]

Covenants of Leadership Behavior

Efforts to lead change are often defeated or sabotaged, not by open and honest disagreement, but by inappropriate, unhelpful, or indirect behaviors. Board members who do not say what they think while sitting at the board table but who hold their opinions only to express them freely in the parking lot after the meeting sabotage what can be done to reach agreement. Leaders who understand their role as a responsibility to fight for their own personal preferences or for the preferences of a subgroup in the congregation force discernment of the future into a win/lose proposition. Leaders who openly share their disagreement with board decisions only after the decision has been made undermine any effective leadership toward change.

When working with congregations that have been experiencing such behavioral barriers to effective leadership and decision making, I often recommend the development of a "covenant of leadership."to uphold. It is not a set of rules that, if broken, will result in a hand slap for the offender. Rules make relationships rigid. They constrain. They limit. Covenants, on the other hand, offer us goals that are in keeping with the values and teaching of our faith. They give us a way to talk about the behavior and practices we adopt in our work together as leaders who wrestle with change and with differences.

When developing a covenant of leadership with a group of congregational leaders, I often begin with some of the problems the board has been experiencing and with some basic information about healthy conflict. The group then develops positive statements about healthy and appropriate behavior around which they are willing to covenant with one another. The list of covenant behaviors becomes a formal, written reminder to the people about the behaviors by which they are seeking to live. Below is an example of a covenant of leadership from one governing board.

A Covenant of Leadership

Our Promises to God

We promise to pray, alone and together, to thank God and to ask
for God's help in our lives and in our work for our church,
and we promise to listen to God's answer to us.

Our Promises to Our Church Family

We promise to demonstrate our leadership and commitment
to our church by our example.
We promise to support our church's pastors and staff,
so their efforts can be most productive.
We promise to try to discover what is best for our church as a whole,
not what might be best for us or for some small group in the
church.

Our Promises to Each Other on [the Governing Board]

We promise to respect and care for each other.
We promise to treat our time on [the board] as an opportunity
to make an important gift to our church.
We promise to listen with an open, nonjudgmental mind
to the words and ideas of the others in our church
and on [the board.]
We promise to discuss, debate, and disagree openly
in [board] meetings, expressing ourselves as clearly
and honestly as possible,
so we are certain the [board] understands our point of view.
We promise to support the final decision of [the board],
whether it reflects our view or not.

This group of leaders wrestled with the specific behaviors and attitudes that were causing them problems in working effectively in their congregation. Their covenantal promises came out of understanding themselves and choosing to practice values and behaviors of their faith that could change their life and work together. Other congregations that have developed covenants of leadership have necessarily developed different lists that speak to their own needs. Each leadership group needs to identify and address the issues and behaviors relevant for them.

The value of such covenants is not in the ability to *enforce* the behaviors. Like any tool of change, the value is in raising the appropriate issues and behaviors to a level of awareness and offering ways to have helpful and safe (nonblaming) conversations about them. Three ways that a tool such as a covenant of leadership can be used for this purpose are:

- Read the covenant in unison at the beginning of a board meeting to remind people of the covenant goals they have accepted for their working life together.

- Spend five minutes in small group or full group discussion of the covenant at the end of a board meeting, asking for descriptive responses to questions such as, How are *you* doing with the covenant? or How do you think *we* as a board are doing with our covenant? or Which of our covenant promises do you think we are struggling with the most?

- Occasionally use monitoring exercises at the end of board meetings. For example, the covenant promises can be easily translated into self-report scales to invite individual responses or reflections. Using a few of the covenant promises above, the scales might look like the following.

- We promise to respect and care for each other.

1	2	3	4	5
We seem to be doing fine with this.			We struggle with this promise and do not fulfill it well.	

• We promise to treat our time on [the board] as an opportunity to make an important gift to our church.

1	2	3	4	5

We seem to be   We struggle with this promise
doing fine with this.   and do not fulfill it well.

• We promise to listen with an open, nonjudgmental mind to the words and ideas of the others in our church and on [the board.]

1	2	3	4	5

We seem to be   We struggle with this promise
doing fine with this.   and do not fulfill it well.

• We promise to discuss, debate, and disagree openly in [board] meetings, expressing ourselves as clearly and honestly as possible, so we are certain the [board] understands our point of view.

1	2	3	4	5

We seem to be   We struggle with this promise
doing fine with this.   and do not fulfill it well.

Use only ten minutes at the end of a board meeting every quarter to have members anonymously respond to such scales. Ask board members to hand in their responses, and summarize results on newsprint for all to see. Board members can then easily see whether there are some covenantal behaviors that they will need to be more aware of or careful about. Or the results may suggest an item for the agenda of un upcoming board meeting.

Covenantal behaviors can be offered to leaders and members alike, not as constraining prohibitions, but as spiritual disciplines of community. If faith communities such as congregations do not wish to default to cultural standards and practices, they will need to practice discipline. Although such disciplines of faith are a part of all our faith traditions, the people of our communities need, and often seek, clarity about which disciplines to follow and how to put them into practice.

Congregations Change from the Middle Out

Although leaders, clergy and laity alike, have a primary responsibility to manage their own behavior and understanding, they also have a dual and direct responsibility to model and mentor appropriate behaviors and learnings in the congregation. Changing the way a congregation thinks and behaves is not a quick and easy exercise for leaders. It means wrestling with learned behavior that people often practice without thinking. Learned behavior and practiced assumptions are natural and ingrained, and for people to behave or think differently will feel unnatural and uncomfortable for a long period of time.

A Game

This is an exercise in preferences, or learned behavior. Alone or in a leadership group, simply follow the directions and pay attention to your responses and feelings.

1. Fold your hands.
2. Now, unfold your hands and refold them—this time with the opposite fingers on top.

Discuss how refolding your hands felt. Could you do it naturally, or did you have to stop and think? Was it as comfortable, or did it feel awkward or odd? Given your preference, with no outside direction, how do you think you will most naturally fold your hands in the future?

This simple exercise demonstrates the power of learned behavior. Although it is possible for people to behave against their preferences and their learned behavior, doing so has an unnatural and awkward feeling to it. New behavior is often difficult to introduce into an organization because of the natural and comfortable feeling that long-term practices carry with them.

Changing the feelings and behaviors of a congregation is changing the "culture" of the congregation, for organizational culture is based on the very assumptions of the organization that give it identity and direct the way it will naturally function. As a consultant to organizations seeking to implement diversity and to change their culture around very fundamental assumptions and practices about gender and race, R. Roosevelt Thomas Jr. states, "Culture change is a long-term process. It takes years, for example, just to establish supportive traditions."[9] Thomas's reference to taking *years* underscores the need for intentional leadership to help a congregation change its assumptions and behaviors around conflict and differences. Changing the culture will require leaders willing to practice the new ideas and behaviors themselves. And then they will need to educate, invite, and offer an observable model to the members in order to engender the necessary changes in the life of the congregation.

It might be helpful to remember that congregations change their behavior "from the center out." Another way of saying the same thing is that leaders change before the members do. If you were to think of the congregation as a series of concentric circles, the leaders (clergy and lay) would be in the center circle. In the next ring would be the active members of the congregation. These are the people who attend the worship services, programs, and fellowship events. In the next circle out would be the inactive people, who do not participate actively but nonetheless maintain a relationship with the congregation. Beyond this circle are the larger community and world in which the congregation lives and offers ministry.

Congregational change does not happen by gathering the larger circles of active, inactive, or community members and offering education or training about the needed change. It begins at the heart of the congregation, within the leadership circle. Leaders need to do the hard and necessary up-front work to understand and develop their own spirits, thoughts, and behaviors, which provide the health and the strength that will enable the congregation to live well with the stresses and demands of change. They need to be clear about the behaviors and practices they will need to change within themselves. They need to covenant with one another to make the change happen. Covenanting makes the intention clear and public. To make your intention public is to invite both *support* and *accountability*.

In a very simple example, the power of support and accountability is seen in the difference between my wishing to lose five pounds and my telling my wife that I want to lose five pounds. When I keep the intention to myself, it is easily lost in old and practiced behaviors that have, in fact, caused me to gain weight, not lose it. But if I tell my wife I wish to lose five pounds, she will provide support to me when she asks how my weight is doing, and I will be accountable when she asks why I chose to order dessert at the restaurant when I was trying to lose weight.

When the necessary up-front work has been done by the leadership circle, the leaders need to "go public" with the larger congregation. It is then time for them to go out into the adjoining circles of members and community to invite changes in the larger congregation. This will, no doubt, require some education and training. In order to see and understand the need for the changes leaders are suggesting, the larger congregation will need to be able to learn what the leaders themselves have been learning. To try to invite change without providing the context and reasons for the change is to invite resistance.

But beyond providing education and training, leaders will also need to *model* the change. They will need to be seen participating in and practicing the new behaviors that are required. If the leaders have developed a covenant of leadership as described above, it is critical that they share the covenant with the members. Sharing the covenant allows the congregation to support and hold the leaders accountable simply by asking how the leaders are doing with their promises. Sharing the covenant also invites the members to practice the same healthy and faithful behaviors. Leaders then have the right to suggest to others that because they are risking new behavior as leaders, it would be appropriate for members outside the leadership circle to do the same.

Although change is always necessary and often exhilarating, it is rarely easy. Change naturally makes us confront the differences in our expectations. It carries with it a feeling of risk. It makes us anxious. But it need not break our relationships. Taking a new position, offering a different opinion, experimenting with a new program, idea, or behavior does not need to be seen as an offense. Leading a congregation in change will inevitably take us into an encounter with differences and conflict. Seeking and risking ways to do this in a healthy manner can lead to a faithful future.

One of the images that has long stayed with me comes from a radio interview with author Norman Mailer during the Vietnam war in the 1960s. When asked why he opposed the war and stood against his government, he replied that he was not against the government. In fact, he said, he loved America so much that it was important to have a "lover's quarrel" with her. Perhaps our providing leadership in change needs to be seen as having a lover's quarrel with a congregation, with a tradition, and with a faith that is sufficiently important and deep-seated in our lives to require the risk that comes with faithful change. Chaplain, preacher, and writer William Sloane Coffin Jr. has provided me with words and images that sharpen my personal understanding and experience of this realization. This Lenten prayer he wrote may serve leaders in a time of change.

> Merciful God, because we love the world we pray now for grace to quarrel with it. O thou, whose lover's quarrel with the world is the history of the world, grant us grace to quarrel with the worship of success and power; with the assumption that people are less important than the jobs they hold.
>
> Lord, grant us grace to quarrel with mass culture that tends not to satisfy but to exploit the wants of people; to quarrel with those who pledge allegiance to one race rather than to the human race. Lord, grant us grace to quarrel with all that profanes and separates persons.
>
> O God of mercy and hope, deepen, we pray, our faith so that we can remain our best when circumstances go against us. Resisting the temptation of melancholy, may we embrace the asceticism of cheerfulness, remaining tender, loving and loyal to one another even as thou art tender, loving and loyal to each one of us. We pray in the name of Christ. Amen.[10]

Exercises for Leaders

1. Discuss with a group of leaders who have read this chapter the following questions:

- What ideas about conflict would be helpful for our leadership group(s) to explore in greater depth?

- How can we structure times to learn about conflict and differences into the regular work of our board and committee meetings, or in a special retreat setting?

2. Using the seven descriptions from the chart of healthy and unhealthy conflict in this chapter, share specific examples—your own or others'—practicing any of these behaviors or attitudes. Reflect together on your conversation.

- Did you more frequently discuss examples from the healthy or the unhealthy side of the chart as you talked about yourselves and your congregation?

- What does this suggest about what might be helpful for you as leaders to learn or do?

3. Discuss within your leadership group the need for a "covenant of leadership." If there is agreement that a covenant would be a helpful tool to develop and use:

A. Describe some of the behavioral problems that you have been experiencing in times of change. You might want to use the discussion from exercise 2 above to identify these problems.

B. Again, using the discussion from exercise 2 above, identify which healthy behaviors and attitudes about conflict would be helpful for you and your leaders to practice in the future.

C. Invite one or two members of your leadership group to *draft-* a covenant of leadership behaviors for the future based on the discussions in items A and B. (This task is best done by one or two people who enjoy writing, because large groups or committees struggle with the task of drafting statements.)

D. Include the redrafting and rewriting of the covenant on the agenda of the board and committee meetings over coming months until you agree that you have identified the necessary and key behaviors on which it will be important to covenant together as leaders.

E. Formally covenant together to practice and jointly review the covenants you have developed.

F. Determine a way publicly to share and model these covenantal behaviors with the full congregation.

NOTES

Chapter 1

1. Fritjof Capra, *The Turning Point: Science, Society, and the Rising Culture* (New York: Bantam Books, 1982), 51-98.

2. Gordon R. Sullivan and Michael V. Harper, *Hope is Not a Method: What Business Leaders Can Learn From America's Army* (New York: Times Business, Random House, Inc. 1996), 3-22.

3. Loren B. Mead, *The Once and Future Church: Reinventing the Congregation for a New Mission Frontier* (Washington, D.C.: The Alban Institute, 1991).

4. "A Conversation with Nancy Ammerman," *Initiatives in Religion* (Spring 1997): 3-4.

5. *Church Membership Initiative: Narrative Summary of Findings/Research Summary of Findings* (Appleton, Wis.: Aid Association for Lutherans, 1993), 3.

6. Sullivan and Harper, *Hope Is Not a Method*, xxi.

7. "The 21st-Century CEO: Senior Executive Insights for Now and the Future," *CSC Index*, 1, El Segundo, Calif.: Computer Sciences Corporation, 1997.

8. Suzanne G. Farnham, Joseph P. Gill, R. Taylor McLean, and Susan M. Ward, *Listening Hearts: Discerning Call in Community* (Harrisburg, Pa.: Morehouse Publishing, 1991), 27.

9. "Caesar's Ghost," *Utne Reader* (August 1997), 32.

10. Warren Bennis and Burt Nanus, *Leaders: The Strategy for Taking Charge* (New York: Harper & Row, 1985), 21.

11. Stephen R. Covey, *The 7 Habits of Highly Effective People* (New York: Simon & Schuster, 1989), 101.

12. Craig Dykstra, "Vision and Leadership," *Initiatives in Religion* 3, no. 1 (Winter 1994): 1-2.

13. *Ibid.*, 1.

14. From Charlotte Roberts, Sherrills Ford, N.C., June 25, 1997.

Chapter 2

1. Charles M. Olsen, *Transforming Church Boards into Communities of Spiritual Leaders* (Bethesda, Md.: The Alban Institute, 1995), ix-xi.

2. Roy Oswald and Speed Leas, *The Inviting Church: A Study of New Member Assimilation* (Washington, D.C.: The Alban Institute, 1987), 15.

3. Roger Fisher and William Ury, *Getting To Yes* (New York: Penguin Books, 1986).

4. Gilbert Rendle, "On Not Fixing the Church," *Congregations* (Bethesda, Md.: The Alban Institute, May/June, 1997), 15-17.

5. Roger von Oech, *A Kick in the Seat of the Pants* (New York: Harper & Row, 1986), 62.

6. Walter Brueggemann, *Hopeful Imagination: Prophetic Voices in Exile* (Philadelphia: Fortress Press, 1986), 3-4.

7. *Ibid.*, 6.

8. *Ibid.*, 1.

9. Ronald A. Heifetz, *Leadership Without Easy Answers* (Cambridge, Mass.: Belknap Press, 1994).

Chapter 3

1. Jeffery S. Stamps, *Holonomy: A Human Systems Theory* (Seaside, Calif.: Intersystems Publications, 1980), 1-9.

2. Edwin Friedman, *Generation to Generation: Family Process in Church and Synagogue* (New York: Guilford Press, 1985), and Peter L. Steinke, *Healthy Congregations: A Systems Approach* (Bethesda, Md.: The Alban Institute, 1996).

3. David B. Goralnik, ed., *Webster's New World Dictionary* (New York: The World Publishing Co., 1978), 1002.

4. Margaret Wheatley, "The Unplanned Organization," *Noetic Sciences Review* 37 (Spring 1996): 23.

5. Lewis Thomas, *Late Night Thoughts on Listening to Mahler's Ninth Symphony* (New York: The Viking Press, 1983), 60.

6. Thomas, *Late Night Thoughts*, 78.

7. Roy Oswald and Speed Leas, *The Inviting Church: A Study of New Member Assimilation* (Washington, D.C.: The Alban Institute, 1987).

8. Ronald A. Heifetz, *Leadership Without Easy Answers* (Cambridge, Mass.: Belknap Press, 1994), x.

9. Arthur Koestler, *The Ghost in the Machine* (London: Hutchinson Press, 1968), 48.

10. David Armstrong, "What is the Proper Object of a Psycho-Analytic Approach to Working with Organizations," a paper presented to a scientific meeting of the Tavistock Center, March 1993.

11. Gary Zukav, *The Dancing Wu Li Masters: An Overview of the New Physics* (New York: Bantam Books, 1979), 29.

12. Walter Wink, *Unmasking the Powers: The Invisible Forces that Determine Human Existence* (Philadelphia: Fortress Press, 1986), 69-86.

13. *Ibid.*, 73.

Chapter 4

1. John Scherer, "The Role of Chaos in the Creation of Change," *Creative Change* 12, no. 2 (Spring 1991): 19.

2. *Ibid.*, 19.

3. *Ibid.*, 20.

4. Answers to the games on page 91.
   #1.

#2   B̶S̶A̶I̶N̶X̶L̶E̶A̶T̶N̶T̶E̶A̶R̶S̶

Crossing out SIXLETTERS produces BANANA

5. Scherer, "The Role of Chaos," 20.

6. Scherer, "The Role of Chaos," 20-21.

7. Fritjof Capra, *The Turning Point: Science, Society, and the Rising Culture* (New York: Bantam Books, 1982), 269-271.

8. Loren Mead, *The Once and Future Church* (Washington, D.C.: The Alban Institute, 1991), 22.

9. Lawrence Kushner, *God Was in This Place & I, I Did Not Know* (Woodstock, N.Y.: Jewish Lights Publishing, 1994), 25.

10. Ronald A. Heifetz, *Leadership Without Easy Answers* (Cambridge, Mass.: Belknap Press, 1994).

Chapter 5

1. Peter L. Steinke, *How Your Church Family Works* (Washington, D.C.: The Alban Institute, 1993), 14.

2. William Bridges, *Managing Transitions* (Reading, Mass.: Addison-Wesley Publishing, 1991), 3.

3. W. R. Bion, *Experiences in Groups* (New York: Basic Books, 1961), 63-65.

4. Joel Kurtzman, *Futurecasting* (Palm Springs, Calif.: An ETC Publication, 1984), 23.

5. William Bridges, *Transitions* (Reading, Mass.: Addison-Wesley Publishing, 1980), 18.

6. Susan Campbell, *From Chaos to Confidence: Survival Strategies for the New Work Place* (New York: Simon & Schuster, 1995), 69-71.

7. Stephen Covey, *The 7 Habits of Highly Effective People* (New York: Simon & Schuster, 1989), 237-238.

8. Speed Leas, *Discover Your Conflict Management Style*, rev. (Bethesda, Md.: The Alban Institute, 1997), 7.

9. Covey, *7 Habits*, 237.

10. Covey, *7 Habits*, 241.

11. Walter Brueggemann, "Conversations among Exiles," *The Christian Century* 114, no. 20 (July 2-9, 1997): 630.

Chapter 6

1. Robert Dale, *To Dream Again: How to Make Your Church Come Alive* (Louisville, Ky.: Broadman Press, 1981).

2. Willis Harman and John Hormann, *Creative Work: The Constructive Role of Business in a Transforming Society* (Indianapolis, Ind.: Knowledge Systems, 1990), 97-98.

3. Marvin R. Weisbord, *Productive Workplaces: Organizing and Managing for Dignity, Meaning, and Community* (San Francisco: Jossey-Bass Publishers, 1988), 70-87.

4. Weisbord, *Productive Workplaces*, 89.

5. Weisbord, *Productive Workplaces*, 71.

6. Calvin Pava, "New Strategies of Systems Change: Reclaiming Nonsynoptic Methods," *Human Relations* 39, no. 7 (1986): 615-33.

7. Pava, "New Strategies," 616-17.

8. Pava, "New Strategies," 617.

9. Pava, "New Strategies," 618.

10. Pava, "New Strategies," 618.

11. Pava, "New Strategies," 619.

12. Yvonne Agazarian, "Functional Management," *Systems-Centered Training News* 2, no. 2 (September 1994): 1.

Chapter 7

1. John Silber, "Obedience to the Unenforceable," *Bostonia* (Summer 1995): 50.

2. Alfred Day, "Widow Stories," *Biblical Preaching Journal 10*, no. 4 (Fall 1997): 19.

3. Stephen Kliewer, *How to Live with Diversity in the Local Church* (Washington, D.C.: The Alban Institute, 1987), 41.

4. Wally Armbruster, *A Bag of Noodles* (St. Louis: Concordia Publishing House, 1972), 5.

5. Dorothy Bass, "Congregations and the Bearing of Traditions," in *American Congregations* vol. 2, eds. James Wind and James Lewis (Chicago: University of Chicago Press, 1994), 172.

6. M.A. Lieberman, I.D. Yalom, and M.B. Miles, *Encounter Groups: First Facts* (New York: Basic Books, 1973), 13-14.

7. Sam Leonard, *Mediation: The Book* (Evanston, Ill.: Evanston Publishing, Inc., 1994), 42-44.

8. Along with this book there are a number of helpful resources that can be used to train leaders, such as:

Speed Leas, *Discovering Your Conflict Management Style*, rev., (Bethesda, Md.: The Alban Institute, 1997).

George Parsons and Speed Leas, *Congregational Systems Inventory* and *Understanding Your Congregation as a System* (Washington, D.C.: The Alban Institute, 1993).

Roger Fisher and William Ury, *Getting to Yes* (New York: Penguin Books, 1981).

9. R. Roosevelt Thomas, Jr., *Beyond Race and Gender: Unleashing the Power of Your Total Work Force by Managing Diversity* (New York: AMACOM, 1991), 59.

10. Leo S. Thorne, ed. *Prayers from Riverside* (New York: The Pilgrim Press, 1983), 36.